Lost Restaurants
OF
ST. LOUIS

Lost Restaurants
OF
ST. LOUIS

ANN LEMONS POLLACK

AMERICAN PALATE

Published by American Palate
A Division of The History Press
Charleston, SC
www.historypress.com

Copyright © 2018 by Ann Lemons Pollack
All rights reserved

Front cover, top left: courtesy of Marilynne Bradley; *top center*: courtesy of Missouri Historical Society; *top right*: courtesy of Toby Weiss/beltstl.com; *bottom*: courtesy of Missouri Historical Society.
Back cover: courtesy of Missouri Historical Society.

First published 2018

Manufactured in the United States

ISBN 9781467140263

Library of Congress Control Number: 2018948044

Notice: The information in this book is true and complete to the best of our knowledge. It is offered without guarantee on the part of the author or The History Press. The author and The History Press disclaim all liability in connection with the use of this book.

All rights reserved. No part of this book may be reproduced or transmitted in any form whatsoever without prior written permission from the publisher except in the case of brief quotations embodied in critical articles and reviews.

*In memory of Joe
who was a joy to share a table with*

Contents

Acknowledgements	9
Introduction	11
Part I: Meet Me at the Fair, and We'll Have a Bite to Eat	13
Part II: Really Golden Oldies	21
Part III: Still Open for Business	101
Part IV: In Those Kitchens	113
Suggested Reading	121
Index	123
About the Author	128

Acknowledgements

The people who helped with this and cheered me on are, as we used to say in health care, TNTC—too numerous to count. I must, of course, begin with the inimitable Joe Pollack, my late husband, coauthor and editor of our three previous books. Joe had an influence on my approach to work like this, among many other things, and has been with me, sometimes at very unexpected times, all through this process.

Alanna Kellogg started me on this tumultuous thrill ride with her suggestion that this project might be something I'd be interested in. She was, of course, right.

Alex Simonovich strolled out of the Way Back Machine and, among other things, gave my search techniques a great boost.

Research for the book turned out to be great fun. The Missouri History Museum's library and research staff were easy to work with, and Jaime Bourassa was of particular help and patience with my efforts. At the St. Louis Public Library downtown, Renee Jones in the special collections area almost read my mind at times. (Gratuitous plug: If you're a history or architecture fan and haven't been in these buildings, you're missing something special.)

Greg R. Rhomberg, nostalgia aficionado extraordinaire, contributed ideas and photos, as well as the suggestion I speak with artist Marilynne Bradley. Marilynne is a jewel and was generous with her art and her ideas.

St. Louis restaurateurs happily shared stories and memorabilia with me. Pam Baroni Neal and Gary Neal of Al's Restaurant and Sherri and Andy Karandzieff of Crown Candy Kitchen talked about their families' heritages.

Acknowledgements

Lisa and the late Fio Antognini of Fio's La Fourchette; Andy Ayers of Riddle's Penultimate; Karen Duffy of Duff's; Chris Laskaris (whose family owned Pelican's Café); Matt McGuire, now of Louie's and former guiding light of the late King Louie's; and William Roth of the West End Grill and Pub were generous with their time and their photographs and memorabilia. Karen Devine, who tended bar at Zinnia, shared good stuff. Joe Hanrahan reminisced about Balaban's. And Vince Bommarito, the dean of St. Louis restaurateurs, had plenty of tales to tell.

Ron Powers took time out from his busy life to offer stories about life at the *St. Louis Post-Dispatch* when it sent him to review restaurants. Senator Jean Carnahan, Kevin Kileen at KMOX, Ella Chochrek at *Student Life*, Julianna Schroeder of the blog *Opulent Opossum*, Toby Weiss of beltstl.com, Paul Hohmann of vanishingstl.blogspot.com and Donald Casalone gave me permission to use pictures—more pictures than we were able to use, unfortunately, but their kindness and generosity are greatly appreciated.

I've been very fortunate to have gone from being an only child to having a far larger family than I ever expected, and they have all been cheering me on. For my Lemons kids, my Pollack kids and the succeeding generations thereof, and for my newest family on both the Maples and the Brewer sides, I send my love and gratitude. Mary Mallory, family in all but technicality, knows where the bodies are buried. Gerry Kowarsky probably has some suspicion about the locations. Mr. T and the Duchess of Escargot gave, as always, general moral support. And my knitting posse gives me Zen and a reminder that there's an outside world beyond food and theater.

Immense thanks to all these folks and many more.

Introduction

If you're reading this, you probably already know that St. Louis loves to talk throwback. And that's what *Lost Restaurants of St. Louis* is. Individual restaurants are the motif here. But I realized at some point that there's actually a story line through it all.

St. Louis is fortunate that it's located in the midst of farms and gardens, a heritage that gave us a head start on good eating early on. The taverns that fed the early settlers weren't getting deliveries from a food wholesaler; fur traders here to sell their wares weren't eating canned stew or freeze-dried corn. The best that the affluent among them might have done was a little wine brought from France or Spain and opened for a special occasion. They were locavores before the word existed.

Things got better as transport improved, sometimes astonishingly so. In the early 1800s, canning was invented. The creation of artificial refrigeration—the first commercial ice maker appeared in 1854—had all kinds of consequences, like barrels of oysters on ice being shipped upriver from New Orleans.

Modernization—we can see the Louisiana Purchase Exposition, our world's fair of 1904, as the tipping point for us—drew us into a new sphere of even easier movement of goods, greater convenience in both foods and kitchen equipment and exotic new cuisines. St. Louisans continue to refer to the fair, but there's so much about it that we've forgotten. The size of the attendance and the huge challenge of feeding so many people are nothing short of stunning. The first section of this book is about the fair and how the guests and workers were fed.

Introduction

After the fair, St. Louis seemed to have gone to sleep. It didn't, of course, but there were a couple of world wars and the Depression, all of which affected dining out. It should be no surprise to learn that restaurateurs were hauled in for selling liquor illegally or violating rationing restrictions. They weren't a bunch of scofflaws, but throughout society, not everyone followed every rule, much less respected it. In the wake of World War II, things began to blossom even more. Lots of restaurants stayed open late, even on weeknights, many more than now. There was still some German food around, but Italian had become more common on menus at places like steak houses. But for the most part, there was relatively little variation in the menus. A few quirks stand out—Stan Musial and Biggie's Steak House offered chopped liver as an appetizer, something we'd only see today at a Jewish delicatessen. Perhaps it was an acknowledgement of braunschweiger aficionados.

Then the stars began to come into alignment. Restaurateurs and would-be restaurateurs stepped up and said, "Why not?" Travel to other continents had become easier, and palates widened. The youthquake that combined an interest in natural foods and a desire for peace in the world mushroomed, figuratively as well as literally. And St. Louis had lots of old storefronts with reasonable rents. All this culminated in what came to be known as the "Class of '72," the five restaurants that *St. Louis Post-Dispatch* restaurant critic (and, much later, in the interests of full disclosure, my husband) Joe Pollack said changed St. Louis dining. Anthony's, Balaban's, Duff's, the Jefferson Avenue Boarding House and Yen Ching all opened. Anthony's had sparkling modern decor and a French-ish menu. Balaban's, too, went French, sort of, casual and beginning to think locally. Duff's was known as the hippie restaurant. Richard Perry's Jefferson Avenue Boarding House was deeply local and offered elevated Midwest granny food. Yen Ching offered Northern Chinese food that wasn't chop suey and chow mein. Things had begun to change.

I include restaurants of all periods here. Some that I wanted to write about I just couldn't find enough information on. A few recipes, requested by many Facebook users, are here, too. I include them with the strong admonition that I have not tested any of them. I've been too busy reading and writing.

But, boy, has it all been fun. I hope you have fun with this, too.

Part I
Meet Me at the Fair, and We'll Have a Bite to Eat

OUR WORLD'S FAIR

The 1904 Louisiana Purchase Exposition is known to most St. Louisans as the World's Fair, almost as though there were no other. It's the benchmark in St. Louis history. Whether that's a bad thing or a good one is open to debate, but visitors aren't here long before they hear about it. Locals usually have some frame of reference to the fair, if only in talking about Forest Park. But most people are surprised when they learn more.

Photographs of the fair are now more commonly seen, so we understand about the elaborate buildings and maybe even the outdoor lighting that so dazzled evening visitors. But hardly anyone now knows the immensity of the project, not just in physical size but in its impact and the logistics required to run it. This was one huge deal, and it's no wonder St. Louis still talks about it, even though we don't quite remember why.

It was about two square miles, roughly the size of Forest Park—although it's not correct that Forest Park was the site. *Part* of Forest Park was the site, and it continued onto what is now the campus of Washington University. There were more than 1,500 buildings. It was estimated that more than 187,000 people attended the opening-day ceremonies, and 25,000 people an hour boarded trains or trolleys to get to the fair through the seven months it was open. Eleven "palaces" of various areas of accomplishment like agriculture and fine arts were opened. Forty-two states and five territories had buildings of their own, as well as sixty-two foreign countries.

Dining on a veranda at the fair. *Courtesy of Missouri Historical Society.*

Apparently, careful statistics were kept (although that didn't prevent some folks from managing to avoid paying the fifty-cent admission). The average daily attendance was more than 87,000. It's not hard to imagine that most of those folks would be there long enough to need at least one meal, possibly more, considering the lure of the magical electric light display at night and the attractions of the Pike, the stretch of amusements that ran parallel to and south of Lindell Boulevard for more than a mile. That was the location of the Ferris wheel, which had a capacity of 2,160 people, camel rides and a Wild West show, for instance. Lots of food, lots of snacks—something not generally accepted in those Victorian times, but no one batted an eye at walking and eating at a fair—and lots of places to sit down were all in high demand.

Food was available at every price level, with various degrees of formality and with an amazing variety of cuisines. The Board of Lady Managers went before the Committee on Concessions to petition for the right to establish simple places where people who brought their own food could sit, have ice water, perhaps buy coffee or tea at reasonable cost and—an important note—"avoid the promiscuous scattering of paper around the grounds." They apparently got at least one such spot; then, as now, the food was part of the experience.

One of the most spectacular was the Tyrolean Alps Restaurant. It was the brainchild of August Busch and his father's good friend Tony Faust. The two of them brought in the noted New York restaurateur August Luchow as a partner. It was not only a restaurant. There was also a sort of ride up to the top of the "Alps," a reproduction of the Passion Play at Oberammergau, a 100-piece orchestra and concerts by choirs twice a day. The main dining room held three thousand people, and the total capacity was five thousand. An outdoor beer garden was offered, the underground cellars holding beer and white wine at one temperature, sparkling wine at another. There were dishwashing machines in the immense kitchen and the only mechanical potato peeler in the United States. Not surprisingly, the cuisine was German, as well as traditional American—sauerbraten and potato pancakes alongside fricasseed turkey wings with oysters. It was the height of elegance, and the prices reflected that. A double sirloin steak with béarnaise sauce was $3.75; newspaper stories throughout the Midwest and beyond told tales of men clutching at their chests when the check arrived.

Just before the fair closed, President Theodore Roosevelt and his wife were honored at a dinner with a banquet for six hundred guests that included oysters, salmon souffle, medallions of beef and risotto with truffles. The intent was for the restaurant to reopen after the fair closed on December 1, 1904, but, despite some legal red tape being cleared, it appears not to have happened. The buildings were torn down in 1907.

The German Wine Restaurant sold only a prix fixe meal for two dollars (about forty dollars today). The food was reported to be superb, and the

Left: The Tyrolean Alps Restaurant. Photo by Jessie Tarbox Beals, the first published female photojournalist in the United States. *Courtesy of Missouri Historical Society*.

Below: East Restaurant Pavilion, where Sarah Tyson Rorer's restaurant was. *Courtesy of Missouri Historical Society*.

restaurant lost so much money that the parent company in Berlin failed and was out of business by the next year.

Other large restaurants included those in the fair's only on-site hotel, the Inside Inn, which held around 2,500 diners; the Old Parliament House in the Blarney Castle exhibit on the Pike, which seated 2,000; and the Italian Cafe, with a capacity of 2,500.

The site of the St. Louis Art Museum was, at the time of the fair, the location of Festival Hall, which had an immense organ. The hall was home to concerts of all sorts. The drives we have now that have been enlarged to parking lots, almost like arms reaching out from the front steps of the art museum, were there then, each terminating in another large, handsome, round building. The East Pavilion Café was the home of a restaurant run by Sarah Tyson Rorer, a cooking teacher and writer and one of the pioneering figures in American food. She was interested in nutrition and cleanliness, and by the time of the fair, she was on the staff of *Ladies' Home Journal* with a monthly column. Her food was classic American, and she served all three meals plus afternoon teas. She also sold a cookbook she had written for the fair, carefully autographing many of them. (For those who are interested, the book is still available on Amazon.com.) The capacity there was 1,200, including private dining rooms on the third floor of the pavilion and a roof garden.

In the West Pavilion opposite Mrs. Rorer's establishment was the Grand Cascade Restaurant, where David Francis, the president of the fair, had his private dining room and where the fair's directors ate and entertained prominent guests.

There were plenty of options at the other end of the price spectrum. St. Louis's own Ralston Purina had an exhibit in the Palace of Agriculture and maintained a lunchroom close by, where everything except the specials were ten cents. The Old Parliament House offered frankfurters and kraut for thirty cents; frog legs were a dollar. A shot of Jameson Dublin Whiskey cost fifteen cents. Will Rogers, by the way, took his wife there on their first unchaperoned date. The evening's entertainment was a young tenor named John McCormack; like Rogers, he went on to greater things. Volney's Quick Meal Restaurant offered both sit-down meals and meals in a bucket, the bucket becoming a souvenir of the visit. Yes, carryout, and the fair's official documents also include the phrase "fast-food" to describe some businesses. The Louisiana and Texas Rice Kitchen on the Pike, sponsored by the Rice Association of America, had hot meals as well as sandwiches, salads and soups. Boiled rice was served free with every meal, there were cooking demonstrations daily, and the souvenir menu included recipes for rice muffins and rice lemon pie, which were, of course, on the menu.

A group of six barbecue stands offered roast beef sandwiches or plate lunches—no mention of ribs, one notices. Ulysses Grant's cabin was purchased by the Blanke Tea and Coffee Company and brought to the fair, where the company's beverages were offered. It's definitely the same cabin that's now at Grant's Farm in St. Louis County. Mrs. MacMurphy's Restaurant for Dyspeptics, run by Harriet MacMurphy from Omaha, didn't have a set menu. In an era when much attention was paid to the gastric system, she said she would prepare food according to the season—less meat in the summer, with lots of both fresh and cooked fruit and salads "if vegetables are available." Across from the bird cage, still in use at the St. Louis Zoo, was the Bird Cage restaurant with open-air dining, allowing patrons to watch the birds.

In an exhibit of the same name, the Anthracite Coal Mine Restaurant was below ground. The walls and floors were made of anthracite coal, and the lunches were Dutch food, served by men wearing miners' helmets with lamps. A large fan like those used in the mines kept the breezes blowing. One of the cars of the Ferris wheel was dubbed "the diner" because many events had been held there when it was rented by private parties. Several weddings were held on the wheel.

Perhaps the most memorable name was the House of Hoo-Hoo Restaurant, located, logically enough, in the House of Hoo-Hoo. Not much is known about the restaurant, but the House of Hoo-Hoo was an organization of prominent lumbermen. The building was a lovely example of Arts and Crafts design with a wide porch almost as large as the main interior room, part of the forestry exhibit and all perfectly respectable.

The fair was amazingly international for its time. Besides the German, Irish and Italian restaurants mentioned, there were Japanese, Mexican, Egyptian, Swedish, French, two Indian, two Filipino, more German and, in the Chinese Village, a chop suey restaurant. The teahouses in the Japanese, Chinese and Ceylonese areas were very popular as places to sit in a comfortable chair, rest a bit, have a nice cup or glass of tea and perhaps a bit of cake or other confection and watch the surge of humanity pass by.

Restaurants and food stands were not the only places offering sustenance on the fairgrounds. There was free coffee from the Brazilian exhibit and the Puerto Rican one, which also had a string orchestra and young women offering the "delicate cups." The Jack Daniel's distillery gave out miniatures. Pillsbury offered baked goods and small sacks of flour, and Log Cabin Syrup

Meet Me at the Fair, and We'll Have a Bite to Eat

The Japanese Restaurant, located on the Pike at the fair. *Courtesy of Missouri Historical Society.*

handed out cans of syrup. Samples of all kinds of things, from oatmeal to gelatin desserts, were given to visitors. In the Minnesota state building, a lunch of pickles, baked beans, bread and butter was available if one arrived sufficiently early. The Walter Baker Chocolate Company, in business now as Baker Chocolate and owned by Kraft Foods, had a two-story exhibit showing how it made chocolate from cacao beans. The smell drew visitors like a magnet. They were rewarded with samples and the chance to buy chocolate and the vanilla extract the company also made. A woman who was a graduate of the Boston School of Domestic Science lectured daily on scientific cooking with chocolate.

The idea of cleaning up the food industry began in the late 1800s, and the Pure Food Movement was in full swing at the time of the fair, a concept the fair organizers encouraged. They allotted two acres for such an exhibit. Sarah Tyson Rorer, one of its most vigorous advocates, utilized her position at the fair to give lectures and hand out pamphlets on the subject.

Folk legend attributes many "firsts" to the Louisiana Purchase Exposition, but our local pride may have gotten carried away. Waffles of different thicknesses were being curled around scoops of ice cream before the combination appeared at the fair. Peanut butter and iced tea predated the fair as well, as did the hot dog, the hamburger and the club sandwich. Many things just getting started made their appearance at the fair and went on to greater things. Dr. Pepper was only made in Waco and St. Louis at that time, and it was sold at the fair. Among the rarities shown were grapefruit and kumquats. A farmer from Houston, Missouri, showed his ginseng, something few had heard of. Turns out there's a variety that grows wild in Missouri. (It's now regulated by the Missouri Department of Conservation.) And then there was the fruit icicle, frozen in a bendable tin tube that could be squeezed to push the contents up so they could be eaten. It's easy enough to figure out what that became. Rice was shot out of cannons to make puffed rice, a technique developed only the year before. Just as amazing was a new centrifuge machine into whose center sugar was poured. Soon, fluffy threads would begin to appear around the edges of the ring. The inventor called it fairy floss. We know it as cotton candy. None of these things were invented at the fair, but the exposition surely brought them into prominence.

At least twelve million people paid to get in, as many as twenty million may have visited, and nearly all of them came across at least one new or exotic food during their visits. And surely they all ate.

It's no wonder we still talk about it. It was far bigger, and more delicious, than we remember.

Part II
Really Golden Oldies

AL BAKER'S

Oh, how the mighty have fallen. Or at least the mighty's real estate. At the northeast corner of Clayton Road and Brentwood Boulevard, where once Al Baker's ruled, there now stands a CVS Pharmacy.

Al and Mary Baker—Mary was very much involved in the restaurant—had sold their interest in Sorrento's on DeBaliviere and took a little time off deciding what they wanted to do. The result was the decision to open a more elegant restaurant than the neighborhood-y spot on DeBaliviere had been.

Opened in 1966, it was indeed very plush—not just white tablecloths and black-tie waiters but chandeliers and red-flocked wallpaper. And Al Baker expected a high level of service from his employees. He stopped serving lunch after a while because he felt that he should be there whenever the restaurant was open, and he wanted to concentrate his attention on dinner. Vacation? The whole place closed for a while every July.

Both the restaurant and its bar, complete with live music, drew extremely well from nearby Clayton's business types, back when Clayton was the headquarters for several national corporations. It became a popular place to meet friends and make new acquaintances, both business and personal. The late, great *Post-Dispatch* columnist Jake McCarthy referred to it as the business card crowd. Often the bar patrons proceeded to the dining room, where they

Dining room at Al Baker's. *Courtesy Clayton History Society*.

sat among regular customers from the nearby affluent neighborhoods and across the area. It also drew celebrities—a large picture of singer Pat Boone held pride of place at one time.

Like most of the leading restaurants in town at that time, there was a certain Italian influence in the menu, offering not just pasta but entrées like veal parmigiana and chicken cacciatore. But there were plenty of steaks, the specialty being a stuffed tenderloin. Baker's was one of the first places in town to serve a wide variety of seafood air-freighted in, and as diners began to look for entrées lower in calories, the restaurant began to offer both steamed and poached preparations. The temptation, however, to succumb to one rich sauce or another may have offset some of the caloric virtue of the fish. An excellent Caesar salad sometimes outsold the house salad, both tossed tableside. In fact, tableside preparation of dishes was another trademark of the house, and some "insider" dishes came only via the guerdon, or cart, that held the burner. The smells and crackles charmed the surrounding tables as much as a musician might. It was, of course, a perfect setup for bananas Foster, a dessert that appeared for a while.

Al Baker was also proud of his wine list, and rightly so. It was remarkably wide and deep, especially in the options for French vintages, the sort of thing that proves that serious attention is being paid to detail. That was Al Baker's standard.

A rent dispute flared with the property's owner, and Al and Mary Baker decided to close on New Year's Eve 1993 and enjoy their leisure.

AN AMERICAN PLACE

Here in St. Louis, restaurants generally hit the big time with home-grown talent leading the kitchen and/or the front of the house. The exception was An American Place. It arrived more or less full-grown under the watchful eye of a big-deal, nationally known chef named Larry Forgione. Forgione had a restaurant of the same name in New York, which was very successful. A disciple of James Beard and his advocacy of American cuisine, Forgione agreed to establish a second location in the old Statler Hotel on Washington Avenue.

The hotel, dark for a while, had opened as the Renaissance Grand in 2003. Its co-owner (with Marriott), a New Orleans–based group called Historic Restoration, Inc., had tried as the hotel was being rejuvenated to persuade Emeril Lagasse to take the space. That didn't happen, of course, and they looked elsewhere. Forgione had some very serious cooking chops and a fine reputation with serious foodologists. He found what he was looking for in the St. Louis property. He told the *St. Louis Business Journal*, "It's rare where it hits every criteria." He continued: "We have a separate entrance and kitchen, a separate receiving area, and a bar. We didn't want to have to be involved in room service or VIP check-ins. Our arrangement allows us to focus on the restaurant."

And it was beautiful—Carrera marble floors, thirty-foot ceilings, a faux-Wedgewood border on the ceiling and pillars restored to their nearly century-old glory made for an elegant dining room with comfortable upholstered chairs and a feeling of serious luxury. It looked, for instance, like the perfect place for a romantic proposal.

Forgione was very serious about gathering the best food for his guests. He could be seen quietly shopping at farmers' markets, mostly unrecognized, and he put his suppliers' names on menus. The food was seasonal, but it was distinctly American. A summer soup of local corn and yellow squash was garnished with chopped roasted poblano chiles. There was also local pork or lamb—he once said the lamb from a farm family west of St. Louis was the best American lamb he'd ever tasted. At the end of the meal, there might be a terrine or a mousse, or the almost casually named "Jim Beard's Seasonal Fruit Shortcake." (It was actually Beard's mother's recipe from when she ran an upscale boardinghouse in Oregon; one can only imagine what *that* fruit tasted like.)

The service was mostly quite good, if occasionally a little errant in its timing. But the staff were flexible. Once, when my late husband and I were at a wine tasting with eight winemakers from Sonoma County, California, which is pretty fine food country, we were asked to find a place that could feed them on short notice. Not just hamburgers, it was explained, something *nice*. A fast phone call to An American Place got us a table at 8:00—at least it was a weeknight—for eleven people. The winemakers were blown away. To our astonishment, they'd never seen purveyors listed on a menu, either. Forgione's folks (he wasn't there that night) did us proud.

An American Place lasted six years, and the decision was made not to re-sign the lease. Washington Avenue isn't quite the same.

BEFFA'S

Long before there were pop-up restaurants, there were underground restaurants. Not restaurants in basements—St. Louis had some of those, too. Underground restaurants were like unlisted phone numbers. (Does that even exist anymore?) You had to know the details before it was of any use. Beffa's was definitely an insider's secret sort of place.

The Beffa brothers, Italian Swiss, began offering hospitality to St. Louis in 1898, first separately near the levee and then together as Beffa Brothers. The following generations took up the ladle, so to speak, moving farther west. In 1966, they made it to 2700 Olive Street, their location across the street having gone up in flames.

It was a cafeteria line—a short one by the standards of the stalwart Pope's or Miss Hulling's. But to find it was a challenge. There was no sign at this location; heretofore there had been. Who knows why? It was not listed in city directories or even the phone book. It closed after lunch service and was only open weekdays. Cash only, please, no credit cards. No spaghetti boards on the wall or even painted menus up there with the mural. And no prices. For years, rumors persisted that different people got different prices. The owners denied it, although, they acknowledged, police and firemen got a break, as did the clergy.

The regulars had the daily specials memorized like they'd memorized their drive to work. Always there was roast beef and turkey and other standards, but corned beef hash—not from a can—was followed by beef stew, green ham (a pork leg that's not cured), chicken à la king and chicken fried steak made the week's lunch menus on regular rotation. Sandwiches with any of those meats, of course, and numerous sides, including deviled eggs, were

Mosaic entrance in front of previous Olive Street site of Beffa's. It is no longer there. *Courtesy Greg R. Rhomberg.*

also popular. The dessert of choice was apparently tapioca pudding, one of those things that folks either love or abhor.

Who were the regulars? A stunning array of local VIPs, who mixed with guys in stained coveralls on their lunch break and office workers from nearby businesses. If there has been a mayor, police chief, fire chief or archbishop of St. Louis who didn't visit here more than a couple of times, it's hard to imagine. Lawyers and politicians shared tables. Senator Thomas Eagleton and theater director Agnes Wilcox were seen, and so were Vince Bommarito of Tony's and cops on the beat. The classic story is told by New York's Cardinal Timothy Dolan. Dolan, of course, was not a baseball player but a Catholic prelate, which is relevant to the story. A native St. Louisan, he tells of walking into Beffa's for lunch when he was an auxiliary bishop here. Who waved him over to join his table? Stan Musial, who was eating with Bob Gibson, Lou Brock and Jack Buck. It was apparently a very enjoyable lunch.

The unwritten rule, it was said, was that one didn't talk about the place very much. Tom Eagleton once said that he'd talked about Beffa's to a reporter—his serving of mashed potatoes was smaller than usual for about six weeks after the story ran. It's also rumored that it stayed open after lunch, something highly unusual, so that one of the city's mayors could hold secret meetings.

But we'll never know for sure. There are some things you just don't talk about. The very discreet restaurant closed in 2016 with little advance notice and no fanfare at all. That's just the way it rolled—for more than one hundred years.

BUSCH'S GROVE

It almost looked like a private home, a very nice farmhouse, except that it was set directly on the road.

Busch's Grove was, indeed, far out in the country when it was built and long before it bore that name. A white frame two-story building with a hipped roof that covered the porch, it seemed very modest indeed for Clayton Road, although it expanded considerably over the years. On the form nominating it for the National Register of Historic Places, it's described as being built sometime between 1855 and 1860. Records are rather fuzzy, but it apparently served as a stagecoach stop, grocery store, post office, saloon and hotel for owner Charles Robyn, who'd bought it in 1873. In 1891, he sold it to one George Buente, who promptly rented it to a fellow named John Busch, who opened a restaurant.

In this area with many German names, there were plenty of Busches. In this case, despite the frequent assumption, he was not related to the Busches who married into the Anheusers, so it was never a brewery property. But the tradition of hospitality was indeed observed, and by the time of the 1904 Louisiana Purchase Exposition, it was a popular spot on a road that led directly to the site of the fair. Long before World War I broke out in Europe, it had a reputation for fine dining and was informally considered an annex to the nearby St. Louis Country Club, the most exclusive of all the clubs in the area.

A long line of movers and shakers frequented Busch's Grove. The neighborhood is one of large lots and generously sized homes, the sort of place where Veiled Prophet queens and corporate presidents live, and for generations, many of them were regular patrons of the traditional American fare, although it was more apt to be lobster than meat loaf. (It did do a fine fried chicken, however.) Additions to the original buildings made for more dining rooms, and a men-only bar was toward the rear. Unique among St. Louis restaurants were the gazebos, often called "the huts," behind the main building. Presumably a refuge from the humid St. Louis summers, with screens protecting against predatory mosquitoes who hung out in the leafy neighborhood before beginning their dusk patrol, they were very popular despite being furnished only with folding tables and chairs. Still, white tablecloths and napkins, of course, and eventually electric fans were provided. Even the main dining rooms were very simple by the standards of the time.

It was a world of signature mint juleps, prime rib and fillet of sole, preceded by tomato juice, fruit cocktail, cottage cheese or a cup of soup, and pie, ice cream or sherbert to finish. (Note the spelling, a usage that may go back to seventeenth-century England.) Busch's Grove was certainly a family restaurant, although at lunchtime it was often full of businessmen quietly doing big deals. Not, of course, just any family. Outsiders, especially in the evenings, were sometimes treated with considerable coolness, and expensive finery helped none at all. But it fed Will Rogers, Charles Lindbergh and, quite often, Stan Musial. There's an apocryphal story about Lindbergh asking where the men's room was. An employee replied, "If you can find your way to Paris alone, I think you can find the men's room."

Another story, far better documented, was about Harry Caray. The legendary broadcaster of the St. Louis Cardinals, then owned by Anheuser-Busch, summoned reporters to the restaurant just after he learned he'd been fired. He sent a waiter across the street to a grocery store to buy some Schlitz beer and made sure it was in the photos that accompanied the interview.

The restaurant closed in 2003. It was purchased by businessman Lester Miller, completely gutted and rethought. Bearing the same name, a sumptuous wine cellar and a whole different menu, to say nothing of Lalique glass door handles, it reopened to fanfare and disagreement from customers, some thrilled, others disputing almost everything about it. It lasted until 2008, when he sold it to a local real estate developer who put a high-end grocery in the building. It's now a self-described "wellness center."

There are still some who sigh nostalgically over the thought of the mint juleps.

CAFE BALABAN

Balaban's? Wait, isn't that still open?

The name lives on in West County, in a spot helmed by Steve McIntyre, one of the two guys who bought the original Balaban's from its creator, Herb Balaban. But we're talking about the first North Euclid spot at the forefront of the Central West End revival, especially when it came to dining.

Most of those of us who remember Balaban's discovered it as a French-ish restaurant using upscale ingredients in dishes we'd only read about. We recall the decor of an old established Paris bistro and a well-heeled clientele with lots of what used to be called bold-faced names.

It was all of those things. But it didn't start that way. In 1972, Herb Balaban, who'd had an antique business on North Euclid at McPherson in a building he owned and then turned into a boutique called the Gypsy Cowboy, inspected the space next door in his building. It had already been a restaurant, including a short stretch as Sarah's, owned by a woman who went on to write for the *St. Louis Post-Dispatch* for many years, Sally Bixby Defty. Balaban decided to open his own place with his girlfriend, Adalaide Dailey, just until they "could find somebody really good to run it."

Despite the political movement of the 1970s, St. Louis was unused to laid-back dining, or dining rooms with gigantic nudes on the wall. The menu was limited; the first night a newspaper critic visited, the entrées were two kinds of crepes. But within a year, it went from 43 seats to 150, and the menu expanded.

It soon became the place to be. "For Rent" classifieds mentioned apartments' proximity to the restaurant. Celebrities in town showed up before shows, after shows or for Saturday brunch—people like Tony Bennett, Isaac Stern, Paul Newman and Bruce Springsteen. One Saturday, Zero Mostel amused a child at his table by blowing bubbles in milk. And yet there were always ordinary people in there, some from the early days, some who'd figured out that regular folks were part of the mix. In 1977, the critic from *St. Louis* Magazine described it as "past its prime."

Critics (mostly) laugh when they're vigorously mistaken, and this was a swell example. When Balaban's, shortly after that description, expanded into an enclosed porch and added breakfast, it brought a whole new dimension to things. (Real croissants! Freshly squeezed orange juice!) Workers coming off night shift at the nearby hospitals could get food far beyond cafeteria dreck while watching Mitch Miller in a business meeting. A disheveled diner, hands trembling but obviously known to staff, nursed a cigarette and a cup

View from the south of the café section of Balaban's. *Courtesy of Marilynne Bradley.*

of coffee before sidling out the door. Somewhere in here, the signs changed to label it Cafe Balaban.

In the midst of this, it became an incubator for St. Louis restaurant talent for the coming decades. While Adalaide was always in charge of the kitchen, she soon acquired a lieutenant who became capable on his own. Lady Charles, Charles Perrine, was a flamboyantly gay man long before "gay" became the term for it. He was a fixture at the restaurant and lived upstairs; any history of Balaban's would be incomplete without his inclusion. He was known for his superb gumbo and his endless supply of sharp, funny remarks. Other folks manning the stove over the years became standouts in other restaurants as well. In no particular order, chefs like David Guempel, Lee Redel, David Timney, Dan Joyce and Andy White were in the kitchen. In the front of the house, Bryan Young, Sean Gallagher, Jack Rinaldi and Ray Sweeney were among the stalwarts; Lady Charles later came out to join them from time to time.

The signature dishes included beef Wellington, a cold cucumber bisque made by Selena Ford before the kitchen officially opened each day and roast duckling. A morel pasta was seasonal before seasonal was chic, and Balaban himself would call certain clients to tell them shad roe had arrived.

A second dining room was acquired beyond the main one. And there was one downstairs in a cellar as well, particularly intimate at night—but of course, it was *always* night down there. Mostly, it was used for meetings and private functions. Occasionally, though, it was a venue for theater with small casts. Very small, in fact, usually one actor, occasionally two, and an audience often with drinks.

There were always high spirits at Balaban's, not just the kind in a bottle or hand-rolled. Late at night, particularly on weekends, merriment often reigned. At one point, the staff decided that they were going to do a homegrown talent show in the style of the by-then-long-gone *The Gong Show*. One contestant, who was quickly gonged out, decided when the idea came up again some months later to be un-gong-able, arriving as Chuck Barris, the emcee of *The Gong Show*, with another employee, who did Gene Gene "The Dancing Machine" (a regular of the show). They were a hit.

In the autumn of 1986, Herb and Adalaide, who by this time were married, decided to sell the restaurant to Tom Flynn, who'd worked there for a long time, and Steve McIntyre, a longtime pal of Flynn's who'd also worked there. They brought in chef David Timney as a partner in 1993.

Herb Balaban died in 2000, and his wake was, of course, held at the "House that Herbie Built." But the difficult times weren't over. His estate sold the building. The untimely death of Flynn in 2001 stunned the restaurant community, but the establishment persevered until 2006. At that time, the business—but not the name—was sold; Steve McIntyre kept the name and owns the West County Balaban's, which is where we began this tale.

CHEZ LEON

Was Chez Leon the closest St. Louis ever came to a French bistro? Maybe. Leon Bierbaum certainly intended it to be that way. He managed to do so very well indeed, without feeling as though it were a Disney version of one.

Located in an old variety store on Laclede Avenue, and then utilizing a narrow former Central American restaurant next door for a bar, it felt right. No cutesy lighting—or at least none that seemed that way. Coat hooks abounded. A row of mirrors on the walls allowed patrons dining with their backs to the room to keep an eye on the action as well as their companions across the table could. Elderly wooden sideboards of unknown provenance held linens and served as work stations. There were white tablecloths and bentwood chairs, of course, and servers in the long white aprons traditional in this sort of setting. It was not quite one of those sepia-toned photographs, but it certainly came close, even in the first year of the new millennium.

In the years before valet parking and sidewalk dining really took hold in the neighborhood, Chez Leon was hopping. And when Leon added them, it got busier. It was easy to stop off before the symphony or after a play, and at least half the time, there was a face or two in the crowd that was identifiable to anyone who paid attention to local media. It might be someone writing or delivering the news or appearing on it, whether an attorney, an athlete or an artist. The hubbub of noise was pretty bistro-like, too.

Leon, not a chef himself but a guy with a fine palate and who at least talked a good game in terms of how he cooked at home, was serious but not grim about food. He certainly wasn't a purist. There was always a hamburger on the menu, and steak frites, so that the conservative eaters were taken care of. Beyond that, it was almost *cuisine grand-mere*, a French grandma's food. Chicken might be roasted or served Provençale, almost always veal and/or lamb in variations, and duck frequently made an appearance in all sorts of roles, whether confit or with olives or a fruit sauce. Cassoulet, the bean-sausage-duck casserole, was a staple every winter. A fine salade Lyonnaise was often found, the bacon-laden salad with a light vinaigrette and crowned with a poached egg. As for the frites, or French fries, Leon was very particular about them. When they were not up to snuff—too much moisture in the potatoes, perhaps, as sometimes happened—he worried and fretted and fidgeted to get them back to wonderfulness. One quite young diner, as she was leaving, informed Leon, who was his own maître d', that the French fries were so good she didn't ask for ketchup. Leon was chortling the rest of the evening.

In many ways, Chez Leon really was his home. He knew many of his customers, and sometimes he treated it like home. One night, he brought in the eminent cabaret singer Steve Ross. It was not a private party, but Leon and Ross made it feel like it was, intimate and casual and giddily high-spirited. Who needs New York's Upper East Side with a night like that?

As is the case with many restaurants, the combination of rent and parking may have been what drove Leon to a location in Clayton in 2010. It was beautiful, of course; he had either a fine sense of aesthetics or of who to call in for help on that score. But the warmth was harder to come by, somehow. Tables were farther apart, the kitchen had occasional glitches and the regulars, many of whom were county residents, didn't come as much. Bierbaum shut it down in the spring of 2012.

DOHACK'S RESTAURANT

For eighty years, the corner of Lindbergh Boulevard and Lemay Ferry Road was home to Dohack's Restaurant. That was even before Lindbergh was called by the name of our town's most famous adopted son, the aviator. Lemay Ferry was named for a ferry across the Meramec River, the southern edge of St. Louis County, run by a man named Lemai or Lemay.

That's relevant, because south of the Meramec, Jefferson County was where the first Dohacks began serving food. Late in the 1890s, they fed steamboat passengers at a hotel in Kimmswick, where the boats tied up for the night. In 1923, the family moved north and opened the family restaurant. The first menu offered ham, hot dogs and barbecue ribs. The family consisted of Joe and Catherine Dohack, their son Ernest, his wife, Josephine, and another son, Art. By 1934, their ad in the *St. Louis Star-Times* proclaimed that they had the largest fish fry in Missouri. They also, in a move foreshadowing today's restaurants, named local suppliers, like Meletio's Fish.

The location was one of the keys to their success. Before the interstates, the highway coming from Memphis, Little Rock and New Orleans, US 61-67, went up Lemay Ferry Road. In its early days, the restaurant was a nice destination for a recreational drive.

As World War II began, the restaurant hosted Selective Service registration sessions, mandatory for men of certain ages. In the postwar years, a 1946 "help wanted" ad for waitresses said Dohack's provided transportation from the city limits, as well as the expected uniforms. People coming into St. Louis from points south, whether en route to shop downtown or to a function, would often make it a point to dine there, returning home talking about the food. It was so well known that a Ford dealership announced in its advertisements that it was next to Dohack's.

Barbecue was only one of the featured items on the menu by then. Dohack's was known for its fried chicken, certainly. But jack salmon was another popular choice. Jack salmon is not salmon, it's whiting—but then it gets complicated. Native son William S. Burroughs wrote about jack salmon, but insisted it was walleyed pike. And whiting is referred to in Baltimore as lake trout, although there it seems to be sold already boned. At Dohack's (where an early menu explained it was indeed whiting) and elsewhere in St. Louis, it's served bone-in, an easily manageable challenge that even a child can rise to. In later years, the Dohack family said that they had originated the name itself. The menu felt home-y; one weekly special as late as the mid-1980s was chicken giblets served with buttered noodles; another was

Dohack's Restaurant. Made of cypress wood, it was destroyed by a fire in 1955. *Courtesy of Missouri Historical Society.*

"American chop suey." Hillbilly bran muffins were a trademark dish. There was even a *Dohack Family Cookbook*.

A major fire destroyed the restaurant, then made of cypress wood, in 1955. Temporary quarters were set up, and a new permanent building opened in 1957. For a while, there were locations on Dunn Road in Hazelwood; in Fairview Heights, Illinois; and in Festus, where the establishment eventually changed its name to Cisco's in an effort to be more contemporary. The fourth generation of Dohacks finally closed the original location in 2003, leaving longtime patrons sighing.

DUFF'S

Once upon a time, the word *hippie* was a noun or an adjective that wasn't pejorative. That seems to have lasted only about six months. It's a shame it came to carry so many negative connotations, because the peace-and-love message that marked the concept as it emerged during the Vietnam War was a good thing.

The cuisine that arrived with it, often vegetarian, was, at the very least, interesting and, with more reliance on natural ingredients and fresh material, seemingly healthy. It always felt sort of free-form, and that was the overall atmosphere at Duff's in the Central West End.

A mismatched collection of furniture and tableware greeted guests when it opened in 1972. The servers assembled by Tim Kirby and Karen Duffy pretty much fell into the same mold. People weren't accustomed to having their orders taken by folks in jeans and love beads, and customers had to have many of the menu items explained to them—"What the heck is a croque monsieur?" And yet it succeeded, soon expanding into the adjacent building (part of the floor forever sloped to the south) and, eventually, into yet the next one. The restaurant debuted unisex restrooms, whose graffiti had to be completely painted over several times to stop the lines of patrons waiting for others to finish reading it.

In many ways, Duff's, another of the "Class of '72" that changed St. Louis's dining habits, was the perfect restaurant, casual but interesting, sufficiently sophisticated to soothe guests from either coast and exotic enough to satisfy the aunt visiting from a small town in southeast Missouri. The menu worked at both ends the same way. Diners could order a simple steak or something like a curry from the Caribbean. During many years of Duff's existence, the kitchen was helmed by Jimmy Voss—at least when he wasn't out on the road feeding the Grateful Dead, something that happened every so often. Brunch was always interesting: a splendid vegetarian black bean omelet with salsa leading the charge, along with pancakes du jour and big, tender muffins that weren't cupcakes in disguise.

Over the years, the crockery and cutlery more or less began to match, and fewer tables required shims under one leg or the other to avoid wobbling. But the restaurant always kept the slightly haphazard aura, even when it was no longer haphazard at all. Well-known faces from around town were often seen at lunch, and weekends seemed always to have one media type or another having lunch or brunch with their family. (A number of those kids ended up busing tables or serving while they were in school.)

Duff's supported its community. Many Monday nights saw poetry or prose readings. William S. Burroughs read here, near his former residence. On a rainy winter Monday, Glenn Savan had the first public reading of his novel *White Palace*. Later, the film of the same name, with Susan Sarandon and James Spader, used Duff's as a Greenwich Village café, with a New York taxi parked outside. After a reading by the late Anthony Bourdain across the street at Left Bank Books, a number of local chefs carried in food for a de facto potluck to honor Bourdain. He, in turn, gave a spirited speech about how important high-quality food is and the chefs' duty to educate as well as feed the public, leaving many of the younger chefs ready to storm the barricades. It was an evening still golden in the minds of those who were there.

When it was about to close in 2013, loyal patrons, some from overseas, returned for one last meal and, in some cases, to see about acquiring a physical reminder. One table that the restaurant had bought from Goodwill had, some years back, been recognized by a customer who'd owned it by a repair he'd done in one spot. He'd given it to a friend, who eventually donated it. When Duff's closed, the customer's daughter took home the table.

A little anarchy in the kitchen is usually a good thing. That's what Duff's proved for forty-one years.

ELSAH LANDING

Elsah, Illinois, is a sleepy village on, and almost in, the Mississippi River. Steamboats once tied up there. Now, the students at Principia College on the bluffs high above the village geometrically increase the population. Nevertheless, it's still small enough that it's just two streets wide, with a village school that closed more than forty years ago. It's a charming, atmospheric spot, and once upon a time, it had a restaurant that was the same way.

In 1975, Elsah Landing opened in part of an old pharmacy built in 1894. Helen Crafton and Dorothy Lindgren wanted something simple that emphasized home cooking. The menu featured soups, salads, sandwiches and pie. Several different kinds of soups were available every day. Both they and the salads were served with half of a small loaf of bread, with a choice of various kinds. But when it came to the pie, that was where the choices widened radically. It was pie, ultimately, that gave the Landing its following, or so it seemed.

It had been popular from the start, and weekends brought lines down the block of people out for a drive on the Great River Road or bicyclists. Parking meant a pleasant walk of a few blocks, inspecting gardens or wildflowers growing out of old stone walls as the diners strolled to or from the restaurant. Inside, it was pleasant, almost Shaker-like in its simplicity, with wood floors, white café curtains, a few tables and a short counter.

In addition to traditional soups, it soon began to branch out to more uncommon recipes that the staff created or found. Beyond the usual were things like cream of lettuce, for instance, or garbanzo hot pot or New Mexico melon. The latter was a cold soup, something uncommon in that period after vichyssoise was forgotten and gazpacho hadn't hit the mainstream. Bread, too, went beyond the usual. But it was the pie that opened the public's collective eyes. Or mouth, really. Yes, the pastry was very good. But what a panoply of options: Williamsburg caramel pie with tart damson plum jam to cut the sweetness; fresh strawberries or peaches (grown nearby in Jersey County) atop a cheesecake-like filling and topped with whipped cream; or the aptly named Scintillating Lemon Pie with two crusts, the top crust cut in wedges, sprinkled with nutmeg and sugar and baked separately. People called to find out when Concord grape pie would be available. Sometimes, a diner would stop by for a piece of pie and then decide to have dessert: another piece of pie.

The bread was sold to take home, as well, so the staff tried cinnamon rolls. Those flew out the door. At one point, they were baking three hundred a day.

In 1981, two things happened: The owners published a cookbook, and they opened a branch in the upscale shopping center Plaza Frontenac. The new location was larger, fancier, not quite the same, although at first the menu was quite similar. In 1984, a second cookbook came out, this one with some additional recipes as part of a section with full-meal menus. By this time, too, the original restaurant had expanded into the other, larger room of the building, more than doubling its capacity. *Better Homes & Gardens* featured it in the autumn of that year, just as the second cookbook was coming into print.

A third cookbook also came into being in 1988, with the recipes being sold as packets. The first packet, which was soups, included a binder to hold the packets.

By 1994, the menu in Frontenac had expanded and gone on to regular entrées for what was a rather different set of patrons. It had already sported a cafeteria line. The partnership ended with Lindgren taking the Frontenac site and, at the request of the center's management during a remodeling, changing the name to Something Elsah. Crafton became the sole proprietor of the one in Elsah. In 1998, she and her daughter moved it to Grafton, Illinois, and ran a bed-and-breakfast in the same building for a few years before it closed.

But the recipes live on. (There's one in the back of this book.)

EUROPA 390

In 1961, there was no Central West End. Oh, the streets were all there, of course, but the concept of it as a specific neighborhood and, more significant to this story, a sort of entertainment district was a good decade off. Frank Mormino would probably have cringed, or worse, at the phrase "entertainment district" to describe where his saloon was located. Gaslight Square was in full blossom, but North Euclid just south of McPherson was a quiet block with some storefronts there at the corner.

His father had owned a series of bars. Mormino played minor-league baseball, joined the Marines in World War II, played more ball when he was discharged and then opened a spot of his own with the late DJ Spider Burks. Called El Capitan, it was at another location. Mormino recalled that he didn't make much money, "but we sure had a lot of fun." In 1961, he rented the storefront at 390 North Euclid for the extravagant sum of $125 a month. (A few months later, he also bought into a business in Gaslight Square as a partner with two other guys. The spot was O'Connell's, but he soon sold his interest.)

It was always a quiet place, focused mainly on drinks, although he served sandwiches that were notably large for the era. They were so large, in fact, that they became the focus of a story that was picked up by wire services and ran across the country: his ability to pile a half pound or so of cold roast beef or ham onto bread.

It was the sort of place that tended to draw regulars. Late one evening, a serious young physician brought a nurse in to have a drink in this place he'd heard about as he assessed her suitability for—well, something. The place was almost empty except for a few guys at the bar. After a while, the couple heard a thud and turned. One barstool, complete with occupant, had overturned. The gents at the bar didn't move. Neither, for some seconds, did the fellow on the floor. No one, including the bartender, acted as though this was out of the ordinary, and the young couple kept their counsel. Eventually, the chap crawled up to a standing position and returned to another stool, ignoring the one on the floor, and the evening went on.

Mormino was always a guy of strong opinions. At times, he was described as being to the right of Attila the Hun, but that may have been dramatic license. He did have some appreciation for the arts. In the early days, several filmmakers working on documentaries and commercials rented offices upstairs and would hang out, guys like Shelby Storck and Pierre Vacho, full of dreams and ideas and stories. Mormino enjoyed their company and the ensuing arguments. In 1982, he utilized the basement for what was known as "Inferno Europa," or The Little Theatre of Frank Mormino, for a couple of plays. And he was good friends with Lady Charles, a flamboyantly gay man who cooked at several restaurants and who lived nearby.

The interior included a sort of balcony in the back, with dark paneling on the walls and what were described somewhere as hazy, "dream-inducing posters," although whether the haze was the result of years of cigarette smoke or the effect of alcohol on the eyes of the beholders was never clear.

Frank Mormino threw in the bar towel in 1987 and went to work as a baseball coach at St. Louis University, returning finally to what must have been his first love.

FIO'S LA FOURCHETTE

Restaurants set their own standards by the way they price themselves. In other words, if you're the most expensive restaurant in town, you'd better be the best. That's a pretty basic calculation. Fio's La Fourchette hit the mark on both cost and quality.

It opened in early 1983. A business story in the *St. Louis Post-Dispatch* wondered if it would be too pricey to last, charging almost thirteen dollars for the least expensive entrée and twenty-five dollars for the most basic five-course, fixed-price meal. It wasn't, and it did.

Fio Antognini and his wife, Lisa, began Fio's La Fourchette in Westroads Shopping Center, where the St. Louis Galleria now stands, in 1982. As per the European style, Lisa Antognini ran the front of the house and Fio the kitchen. Both were Swiss. The result was a mixture of cultures, like Switzerland, including some things distinctly different from any of the "parent" influences.

Probably the strongest current on the menu was classical French, evolving under Fio's imagination into new and different choices. By the time they moved to a Clayton location near the old Famous-Barr in 1994, entrées could be things like fork-tender veal in a rich reduction of wild mushrooms or venison with a gingery pineapple salsa, the latter from a reduced-calorie menu as far from punitive as could be imagined. In the European style, salads followed the main courses.

When people reminisce about the restaurant, two things are always mentioned. One is souffles, three options every evening, always the chocolate,

Really Golden Oldies

Exterior of Fio's La Fourchette's Forsyth location. *Courtesy of Fio and Lisa Antognini.*

Fio and Lisa Antognini. *Courtesy of Fio and Lisa Antognini.*

because Swiss pretty much equals chocolate, of course, and other rotating choices. The second memorable thing is that, while servings were small by St. Louis standards, servers always offered seconds, not just to VIPs but to all patrons.

And VIPs there were. In 1984, Yul Brynner did four weeks at the Fox Theatre and came in every week. Everyone was treated just as royally as was the star of *The King and I*—politely, but with just a touch less stiffness, somehow, than some places in this price range. There were plenty of proposals and plenty of special dinners, like a much-anticipated annual wild-game dinner.

One New Year's Eve, there was a widespread power outage as the second seating began. The fire department wanted the restaurant to close down, but Fio and Lisa persuaded them to allow things to go on with candlelight and flashlights, gas powering the kitchen stoves and multiple employees standing by with fire extinguishers. No one forgot that night. We'll bet all the firemen got souffles as thank-you gifts.

Fio's La Fourchette closed in 1991. Fio was always interested in the world beyond his kitchen, too, activities like team parachuting. They retired and ended up in Utah, returning to St. Louis for private dinners and some wine dinners. Fio passed away far too soon in May 2018 in a rock-climbing accident. Souffles will always bring him to mind.

GIAN-PEPPE'S

Among the old-school white-tablecloth restaurants on The Hill, Gian-Peppe's was a sort of nova, one of those stars that appears, flares brightly and then disappears. It lasted from 1981 until around 2001 in a relatively small spot on Marconi Avenue. It was, as such places often are, a family effort.

The Profeta family came to St. Louis in 1977 with a background in restaurants. Dad Salvatore had worked in restaurants all his life; mom Gabriella's four brothers all worked in restaurants. Once in the United States, they worked and saved and learned English for four years. Finally, there was enough money to buy a house or start a restaurant. Sal opted for the restaurant. Peppe, their eldest child, said, "Dad's a gambler. And it turned out well for us." (The name of the establishment is Gian, for Salvatore's middle name, Giovanni, and Peppe for the son.)

Indeed, it did. While the decor was elegant, and the waiters were in black-tie, it seemed less formal than many of its peers. The late British actor, writer and noted trencherman Robert Morley said, "No man can be lonely while eating a plate of spaghetti." That was the feeling: one plate of pasta, and you were a friend of the house.

Gabriella ran the kitchen and turned out home cooking of the most elevated kind. Fine soups included a chicken soup that would put antibiotics to shame with its curative ability, and there was a careful hand with calamari, whether fried or in a tomato sauce, all to kick off an evening's dinner. Sister Debora made the salads, and the other sister, Nadia, was the hostess. Peppe worked both the back and the front of the house and was a dab hand at both. Pasta carbonara, he would occasionally proclaim, was his favorite. "I've been making it since I was a kid!" He preferred to use bucatini, long, hollow strands that kept their texture.

They prided themselves on the veal dishes, but the real strength of the house seemed to be in the respectful way seafood was treated, whether as an appetizer or a main course. It was one of the few restaurants in the neighborhood that served dinner rolls—warm ones at that—instead of bread with meals. It also had a traditional dessert from Calabria, in southern Italy, called a *tartufo*. That translates as a truffle, but the dessert is a ball of ice cream, pistachio in the case of Gian-Peppe's, encased in a hard chocolate shell, sort of an Eskimo Pie for adults. If they ran out of Gabriella's tiramisu, as they often did, it was almost as good.

Within a year, the restaurant was extremely popular, and reservations were a must. One transplanted Bostonian took a date to Gian-Peppe's soon after the restaurant had gotten its first big review. Not understanding what a mistake it would be, he hadn't called ahead. They waited an hour before he admitted defeat. The lady led him to another place for dinner.

The closing in 2001 was very quiet, but Peppe Profeta is still working in St. Louis, charming people and encouraging pasta carbonara and other good things.

GRECIAN GARDENS—TWICE

This story will be a double feature, a phrase not heard much anymore. It meant that one admission to a movie theater would get the customer two different films (plus cartoons and a newsreel, but we won't include that here). This is about two different restaurants called Grecian Gardens.

If you remember double features, then you might be old enough to remember, or at least remember hearing about, Jim Mertikas's Grecian Gardens at 205 South Sixth Street. Jim's last name seemed to get conflated with the liqueur mastica, flavored with resin; after a while, the restaurant was sometimes referred to as Mastica Jim's.

Mertikas opened the restaurant in 1918, and it became popular with visiting sports types and other celebrities. Lots of signed photos lined the dining room proclaiming the virtues of his restaurant from people like Jack Dempsey, the famed boxer. A letter from President Franklin D. Roosevelt thanked Mertikas for a gift of *koulouria*, the Greek Easter bread. In those days, people stayed out late, and it was known as an after-theater spot as well. "Air cooling" was installed in 1934. Mertikas was also known for hosting charity dinners for Greek relief in the years before and after World War II.

He learned in the kitchens of the Southern and Jefferson Hotels and offered both Greek and American food, although there are numerous reports that at least sometimes, when new guests asked for a menu, his response was, "Eat what I bring you. It's good for you." Newspaper advertisements for the restaurant talked about chicken, steak and squab. Sometimes, this latter word is used for a very young chicken rather than the all-dark-meat young pigeon it originally meant, but we'll never know which bird was appearing on these tables.

To be sure, there was plenty of alcohol around, even during Prohibition, when Mertikas was fined for serving it. The signature drink was a "Call Me Charley," which involved placing a sugar lump and some lemon juice in the mouth before downing a slug of brandy (we suspect Metaxa, the Greek brandy) or gin.

He passed away in 1958, and the restaurant was taken over by Edward Kelly, who had been a St. Louis policeman. But without its host, patronage fell off drastically, and it closed in 1961.

The other Grecian Gardens opened on Euclid just south of Laclede in 1970. Located on the bottom floor of a low-rise apartment building, there were two sections, the dining room on the right of the entrance foyer and the bar on the left. It was run by Pete Georges and his brothers John and George, plus more family when it first opened. Pete had been a part owner of the old Rex Café, a stalwart of Gaslight Square in its early years. But this was no diner.

The dining room took itself pretty seriously—white tablecloths and black-tie waiters, especially the remarkable Aris Papadimos. Aris was the guiding spirit for newcomers to this cuisine. He guided customers to good choices, such as not choosing two dishes with the same sauce and warning the unsuspecting about drinking *retsina*, the Greek wine flavored with pine resin. Kind and gentle and funny, he was capable of being dignified when the customers seemed to expect that sort of treatment. Eventually, he'd win those folks over, too, with his charm.

There were some run-of-the-mill choices of steak and seafood, but most of the menu was devoted to real Greek food cooked by real Greeks. By contemporary standards, it was very retro, because no one made any fuss over *saganaki*. The flaming dish and shouting of "Opa!" apparently came out of Chicago's Greektown. Instead, saganaki arrived bubbling on a metal dish, hot from its time under a hot grill, tangy from a last-minute squeeze of lemon juice. The slightly coarse bread was made in-house. Salads were fresh and crisp, with oil and lemon juice and oregano, plus the new-to-most-of-us cheese called feta. The lamb for the kebabs was of a high quality, and there were things like stifado, the beef stew, and moussaka, the casserole with lamb and eggplant, as well as chicken broiled with lemon and oregano, oregano being the most Greek of herbs.

Of course there was baklava. But more interestingly, there were Greek wines that weren't resinous, like *roditys*, the dry rose, or *demestica*, a red. Both were sharp and exuberant, just the thing to match with this food. Vintage? The *Post-Dispatch* reviewer opined that if someone had asked about the vintage, Aris would have looked thoughtful and then said, "June was a good month." After the meal, there was the thick, sweet coffee in espresso cups, intense and bracing. When I returned to the restaurant once after a vacation, complaining that the Greek coffee I'd found was not up to the Gardens' standard, Aris taught me how to insist that the coffee be served *glykos*. The instruction has served me well over the years, despite servers' obvious astonishment at seeing my noticeably Anglo-Saxon self emphatically using the Greek word for "sweet."

The other door in the foyer led to the bar, dark and cozy until the weekends, when there would be Greek music from a bouzouki band. Sometimes, a belly dancer graced the floor, but that was secondary. The crowd, often family groups, would dance to the music, doing the syrtaki and other traditional dances. Outsiders were welcomed and encouraged to get up and join in. Regular customers who were female and who ventured into the bar weren't made to feel uncomfortable. Instead, unwelcome attention was shooed away by Aris or one of his associates, although occasionally an exception seemed to be made for a man whom they deemed suitable for the woman in question.

The restaurant closed in 1975, despite an effort to become more casual, including placing what may have been St. Louis's first gyro spit in the foyer, so that the sight and smell of it were noticeable on the street. If one listens closely on a quiet night near the former entrance, the sound of a bouzouki might still be heard.

THE GREEN PARROT INN

The Green Parrot Inn was known for its fried chicken, its honey butter for hot yeast rolls and its parrot. Located in a stone house that was originally a private residence built by William Bopp around 1915, it was, for a while, a speakeasy, one of those establishments that served alcohol when the Prohibition era created by the Eighteenth Amendment to the U.S. Constitution made it illegal to do so.

Tena May Dowd had opened a successful restaurant in Wichita. She moved it to Kansas City when her husband was transferred, and then, with her brother James Toothman, decided to open one in St. Louis. The building was purchased in 1938 and operated by Toothman and his wife, Mary, who had gone in on the deal with Mrs. Dowd.

Of course, there was a parrot. The large cage was on the enclosed porch where guests entered to eat at one of several dining rooms. In the days before Colonel Sanders rode roughshod over mom-and-pop chicken restaurants, it was a particular pleasure to have someone else standing over a skillet of hot lard crackling and bubbling as the chicken got to just the right golden hue. It proved to be a big hit, and some St. Louisans still remember it as a place for a special meal or a big occasion like a holiday or graduation. Well-behaved children were rewarded with a stick of chewing gum when they left. One nostalgic local called it "the place where I learned to eat out."

By 1951, there appears to have been some sort of falling out, because an ad announced that the Green Parrot "operated independently of any affiliations or branches." But the Toothmans and their next generations continued their work there. At some point, a mynah appeared in a cage near the eponymous parrot.

The menu, pretty much unchanged over the years, was headed up by the fried chicken, although there was also a steak option. It was preceded by a green salad and accompanied by mashed potatoes, of course, cream gravy, "Spanish rice, cottage cheese, green fresh vegetables, applesauce, hot rolls, fresh butter, preserves and dessert." Dessert was ice cream or sherbet; for an extra fee, pie was available, chocolate being particularly popular.

Around 1962, the menu expanded slightly and the ads began to politely point out that swordfish steaks and lobster tails were being served, as well as Hungarian apple and cherry strudels. But the no-alcohol policy continued; as late as 1977, it was still in effect, according to a review in the *St. Louis Post-Dispatch*, which said the Toothmans believed "good food and alcohol don't mix."

James Toothman died in 1962, and his wife, Mary, passed away eleven years later. Their sons took over running it, with Ben buying out Elmer in 1978.

The restaurant closed in 1983. The Toothman family said they served eight hundred diners the last day of service. A dramatic slowdown in business caused the closing, an immense change from the time when it did sixteen hundred meals on a Sunday during World War II—no small accomplishment given gasoline rationing. The parrot, perhaps sensing what was afoot, had died three weeks earlier.

A recipe from the Green Parrot Inn for its fried chicken is in the last chapter.

HARVEST

Do you remember how hard it was to get a table at Harvest? For a long time, it was the hottest ticket in town. It booked six weeks ahead, and people were happy to get even a 5:45 reservation on the night they were aiming for. Located in the north half of a building on Big Bend Boulevard in Richmond Heights owned by Hank's Cheesecakes, it exploded onto the scene in 1996.

That spot had a certain history to it. Longtime St. Louis eaters know that Harvest was located in Cyrano's second location. Cyrano's was an atmospheric coffeehouse with desserts and sandwiches, although the latter seemed an afterthought. For a generation, it was a date night or an after-theater stop. For many years of Harvest's existence, guests would walk in looking as though they'd fallen down the rabbit hole, expecting to find Cyrano's Cleopatra Sundae.

There was no question about it. Harvest was serious food. Not grim, mind you; there was nothing stuffy about the place, but the two chefs that started the kitchen, Steve Gontram and Matthew Bousquet, had come from San Francisco with impeccable resumes. Chez Panisse, Postrio—places like that. They entered into a partnership with Bob Gontram (Steve's dad), Charlie Downs and George Mahe. It was American food with fresh local ingredients sometimes bought from farmers who showed up at the back door. (Mahe muses about one purchase of $400 worth of yellow chanterelle mushrooms.)

Not only did it taste good, both the familiar and the not-so familiar dishes, but it also was served in quantities that St. Louisans would appreciate. The restaurant knew St. Louis diners wouldn't enjoy three brussels sprout halves arranged on an artful smear of red pepper coulis, no matter how delicious they were. Along with the esoteric, like hanger steaks, salsify and cardoons, came dishes like a magnificent pile of French fried onion rings with a cayenne-tinged blue cheese dipping sauce. It was a great mix of possibilities to charm all but the most gastronomically hesitant.

Steve Gontram tells the story of a man in the dining room who was loudly complaining about a popular dish. Halibut was roasted in a polenta crust until the cornmeal mixture was golden and the fish was just cooked through. The fish, the man said bitterly, was terribly old, mushy and tasteless. Gontram, who dressed most of his seafood himself, came to the table carrying the frame, or skeleton, of the sixty-five-pound halibut and discovered that the fellow hadn't even forked through the polenta to get to the fish.

The two-level dining room, complete with fireplace, seemed to be rocking constantly. The tables by the fireplace were the most requested, but the ones by the railing of the upper level with a view of the room were the best place to watch the floor show that a busy restaurant always presents. Even after the new wore off, it stayed hot for a long time, a favorite spot for business dinners, wine tastings and hordes of Washington University parents anytime there was an excuse for them to be in town.

St. Louis was so satisfied with Harvest that when New York restaurateur and former St. Louisan Danny Meyer was quoted in *Gourmet* magazine saying Harvest was his preferred special-occasion restaurant locally, it hardly caused a ripple, except, of course, among the restaurant staff. In 1998, Gontram served Thanksgiving dinner at the James Beard House in New York, a significant honor that took a year of preparation. Jean-Georges Vongerichten, the big-deal New York chef, quietly came to that meal.

And about those folks who came in thinking they were at Cyrano's? "If we could get them to try the bread pudding, they were always glad they stayed," says Gontram. In fact, Carolyn Downs, the wife of partner Charlie Downs, who made the bread pudding, went on with her husband to open the new version of Cyrano's, now in Webster Groves, as well as Sugarfire Pie.

The Gontrams, who had bought out their partners, sold the restaurant in 2010. It began to lose steam and finally closed in 2014.

THE HOUSE OF MARET

It started as a gas station.

The House of Maret was on land that had been homesteaded by Wilhelm and Barbara Maret in 1871. Eventually, the area would be part of what came to be Sunset Hills, long before the street was called Lindbergh Boulevard. Two generations later, one of the Marets was running a small gas station on the property. In 1930, he began selling what the family called "simple tavern food." Soon, a dining room was added, which featured barbecue. Robert Maret came out of the U.S. Air Force in 1953 and not long thereafter went into the family business. The gas station was sold; the tavern-restaurant was popular as a "well-known roadhouse," said Maret. The college kids, he went on, liked to come and dance.

He, however, clearly had aspirations for something a little more sophisticated. He turned it into a large, elegantly appointed place that seated around three hundred. There were plenty of stained-glass windows, four fireplaces and wood-paneled walls.

Stained-glass window at the House of Maret.

The outdoor garden was an immense source of pride to the family. A brick-floored patio surrounded a large fountain, and pots of tropical plants were added to in-ground plantings when the weather turned warm enough. It was, of course, used for outdoor dining, and on some Saturdays, weddings were held there. At least once, a garden club met there to hear a discussion on commercial landscaping—and, of course, to admire the Maret garden and have a nice lunch.

German dishes headed up the menu. Sauerbraten, hasenpfeffer, wiener schnitzel, roulade and, of course, sausage led the way with potato pancakes, red cabbage and spaetzle as sides. There were always a few steaks and some seafood, but also at various times duck in orange sauce and boeuf bourguignon were listed as "European specialties." Breakfast was served, and that's the word that was used, even on the weekends. Apple strudel for breakfast? What a brilliant idea!

The Maret family sold it in 1988. In a twist of fate, it became a barbecue restaurant.

IN SOO (FORMERLY SHU FENG)

"Hold it by the bottom!"

For a large number of St. Louisans of a certain age, this instruction, delivered in a loud voice, will evoke a big smile and a sudden onset of salivating.

There is still a restaurant called Shu Feng, in the same place as Shu Feng began. But in the way that small Chinese restaurants or, in this case, Chinese-Korean restaurants do, things changed. The restaurant moved out to Chesterfield, then came back. There were a couple of periods of it being closed, during one of which the name was sold to someone else.

That Shu Feng opened, raising hopes among the many fans. But while nice enough, depending on how polite the original fan was in conversation on the topic, it wasn't the right Shu Feng, name and address notwithstanding. Finally, In Soo Jung and her husband, Steve Fung, opened a place a few doors away and called it In Soo.

Confused? Yes. The dates of all this happening are lost in the mists of time and perhaps some real estate records. The original Shu Feng seems to have opened in 1983 or 1984. The first closing ended in 1994 back at the old location. By 2002, In Soo was where the action was set up and running. It closed in 2009. But the memories of In Soo and In Soo's food are probably why everything else about it is of secondary importance.

Soo ran her dining room with a firm hand. Someone compared her to Margaret Thatcher. Actually, she wasn't quite that stern, especially once she got to know the customer. Nevertheless, she had strong opinions on where jackets should be hung, how much to order and how much care should be taken of carryout food. As to the latter—that was the basis of her trademark phrase. Apparently, in the early days, someone had been careless and the brown paper bag was flawed or perhaps it had just been overpacked. Whatever the cause, the bag had given way, and the customer complained. There is no clear story of the consequences other than her perpetual reminder to every single customer carrying out dinner or just leftovers, the reminder often flying across the restaurant before departure. Hold the bottom. Don't waste the food.

Because it was the food that people came back for, that people moaned about missing when it was closed and raced back to glory in again when the doors reopened. Foremost, at least in my mind, were the water dumplings. Boiled dumplings, not potstickers, were so juicy that one wonders if they were related to the soup dumplings, *xiao long bao*, that have become a staple in Shanghainese restaurants, although smaller. Always seemingly cooked to order, with the soy/black vinegar sauce on the side, they thrilled. The hot and sour soup was rich and perfectly seasoned, not inflammatory but spicy and wondrously tart. People swore by the *moo shu*, which came in five varieties. There was also stir-fried string beans with or without meat, crispy fried eggplant in spicy sauce, and if garlic was needed, there were the Korean specialties on the back of the menu, starting with *bulgoki* and going on to the kimchee-seasoned dishes. We wonder what Soo would make of the current fancy chefs' interest in kimchee fried rice.

The restaurant was sold to new owners in 2009. But in what other defiantly non-fancy restaurant would one have seen this: A Tuesday night in the restaurant found Al Baker, the restaurateur; Don Wolf, an attorney and jazz disc jockey; Senator Tom Eagleton, an eater of no small abilities; and the food critic for the *Post-Dispatch*. Not at the same table, just all ready for some good food and carefully carrying home the inevitable leftovers—holding them, of course, by the bottom of the bag.

IRV'S GOOD FOOD

The Missouri Botanical Garden is a fine place. It's respected around the world, and it tries hard to be a good neighbor to the homes and businesses around it. Nevertheless, Irv's Good Food is gone, replaced at the northwest corner of Vandeventer and Shaw by a parking lot for the garden.

In living memory, Irv's was always, uh, unassuming. In its last years, it would probably be classified as a dump. It had mostly stools, a few booths with torn

LOST RESTAURANTS OF ST. LOUIS

Irv's Good Food. *Courtesy of Marilynne Bradley.*

leatherette, but it was open all night. The door was always locked after a certain hour, but I never heard any reports of anyone being turned away. They knew the crowd would come after the bars closed on weekend nights.

St. Louis didn't have diners in the style of the Eastern Seaboard, with the old railroad cars and the aluminum prefab buildings made to look like railroad cars. Our diners were white-tiled, freestanding buildings or those same façades tucked into a corner of an office building in an older neighborhood. Early in its existence, Irv's had carhops, but those disappeared eons ago, leaving a large parking lot for the after-hours crowd or, later in the morning, the folks who needed a quiet breakfast, perhaps because they were part of that same overindulgent group.

Irv's served breakfast at its most elemental: biscuits and gravy; white toast slapped with butter or something like butter; thin strips of bacon; eggs, always eggs. Because what self-respecting spot like this would have a grill man who couldn't cook eggs correctly?

Then there was the "Nightmare." No, not the landlord who wouldn't renew the lease in 1999. The Nightmare. It was Irv's phrase for a slinger,

St. Louis's ubiquitous and unique challenge to the gallbladder. Potatoes to start with. Before we called them hash browns, before the annoying generic phrase "breakfast potatoes" ever saw daylight, there were just potatoes on a breakfast menu—fried, sometimes hashed, not deep-fried. So, potatoes. Then a sausage patty, maybe two, or perhaps hamburger patties. Then eggs, probably best as sunny-side up or perhaps over easy, but some folks insisted on scrambled. The dish was topped with a ladleful of hot chili. Cheese? Maybe. Chopped onion? Why not, at this point? The theory has always been that it soaked up alcohol. Generations of St. Louis University undergraduates tested the theory over and over again. The results were never published in any scientific journal, so who knows what they found?

But the jukebox played, and someone's forgotten, faded jacket hung on the coat rack. It lasted fifty years before Irv's went away.

JACK CARL'S TWO CENTS PLAIN

Everything came with a side of tongue at Jack Carl's Two Cents Plain delicatessen. Jack was a native St. Louisan whose father had owned a delicatessen in University City. Nevertheless, Jack's skill at repartee equaled anything found behind a meat slicer in Manhattan. His older brother Bill, who eventually moved the family business to Clayton, was apparently the calm one. Jack? Not so much.

Actually, he was a nice guy, but the shtick worked. He opened the original Two Cents Plain on Clayton Road in the postwar years but moved to Gaslight Square in 1960. While the area seemed to specialize in entertainment for grownups—live music, bars, good restaurants, a coffee house or two—it made sense to have somewhere that folks might stop with their families to have a bite during the sightseeing or for businessmen to have lunch. Enter pastrami, carved by Jack.

It was never a kosher restaurant. It was sort of kosher-style, but at some point, Swiss cheese appeared on a corned beef or a pastrami sandwich. That put an end to any hope at all of kosher-esque. There was always matzoh ball soup and various types of smoked fish and, of course, bagels. That was a big deal then; you could buy cream cheese anywhere, of course, but to find a bagel, you had to get to a Jewish delicatessen or a Jewish bakery, uncommon anywhere but a certain area of town. (The delicatessens sprinkled all over South St. Louis were actually small corner grocery stores with meat counters. Consider the word *delicatessen* a gift from the German immigrants of the mid-1800s.)

It's hard to imagine how many folks had their first taste of that kind of food under Jack's eye. Business was good enough that the year after he arrived in Gaslight Square, a pastrami war broke out when his landlords, saloon owners both, decided to drive him away by offering cheaper sandwiches. If he left, they must have thought, they could use the space themselves. Liquor brings in more money per square foot than pastrami and coleslaw. Jack Carl won and kept feeding people, along with his trademark line of patter.

It wasn't always a Don Rickles–type insult. The odds were higher that it was, though, if the customer were a man. When the delicatessen moved downtown in 1968, there were plenty of attorneys and other courthouse types undeterred, indeed invigorated, by the banter. The proprietor was also never short of an opinion as he continued to slice meat and make huge sandwiches in the new site, whose walls were covered with a multitude of photographs and other memorabilia, all moved from the previous locations.

Jack Carl was sufficiently eclectic to stock German and Italian salami alongside the kosher brands; he carried the St. Louis–made Volpi sausages with considerable pride. Actually, he was a fair gourmet and cheerfully reported back on his latest trip to New York or transatlantic crossing—he was a big fan of the Cunard ships—and gave interested customers serious reviews of his gastronomic wanderings.

His fans came from all walks of life. Milton Berle came in regularly for the tongue—the kind that came on rye bread with mustard, although probably plenty of the verbal sort as well. Senator Abraham Ribicoff (D-Connecticut) came as well, as he didn't like the food at the now-defunct Jefferson Hotel where he was staying. Jackie Mason was such a patron that Carl suggested they name the federal courthouse after him because it would bring in more tourists. He considered franchising the delicatessen and opened branches in Northwest Plaza and in Clayton. There was a brief move back to the Gaslight Square neighborhood, a return to downtown and, finally, a place in the 1100 block of Olive Street, still very close to the courts.

Photos of all those folks and more were on the walls. There was also one of a stripper named Jada. There are a couple of versions of the story about what happened the day she ate at Jack Carl's Two Cents Plain. She was working at the long-gone Grand Theater on Market Street. She had been employed as an ecdysiast, too, at one of Jack Ruby's clubs in Dallas the weekend of the Kennedy assassination, when Ruby killed Lee Harvey

Oswald on live television. The day of Jada's visit, Ruby's trial was expecting a verdict. A Dallas sportswriter named Bud Shrake (who eventually became the companion of Governor Ann Richards toward the end of their lives) had suggested at one point that Jada call a friend of his when she came to St. Louis. She did, and when Shrake's pal picked her up for lunch, her radio was on. She wanted to wait to listen for the verdict in Ruby's trial. The jury was already out, and the guilty verdict came quickly. Jada, reported the gentleman, howled like a triumphant animal at the news. Ruby was, she said, an absolutely terrible man to work for, cruel and cheap. The two of them proceeded to go to lunch at Two Cents Plain, and Jada left a signed photograph for the wall.

Jack closed for the final time in 2005. He presented the photograph of Jada to her lunch date that day, whom I had married decades afterward. It remained in our house until my husband's death. Joe was, among many other things (but after the time of the visit with Jada), the theater and restaurant critic for the *St. Louis Post-Dispatch*. William Roth, owner of the West End Bar and Grill and the Gaslight Theater, located very close to the original Gaslight Square intersection of Boyle and Olive, came to me and asked if there was anything I might have that they could put up as a memento of Joe. And so the picture of Jada is back on the wall of a restaurant, smiling as people eat. It remains there today, even though there are no pastrami sandwiches, with or without cheese, on the menu. There is, thanks in part to the theater crowd that hangs out there, plenty of tongue—the verbal kind.

JEFFERSON AVENUE BOARDING HOUSE

It's surprising how fast Richard Perry's Jefferson Avenue Boarding House has left the collective memory of many St. Louis eaters. It wasn't large, certainly, although the storefront on South Jefferson at Utah eventually expanded to a second dining room. Decor, however, was far more lush than one would anticipate. Perry opened the restaurant in 1972, with food very different from what St. Louisans expected. It wasn't a formal restaurant, but Perry was very serious about midwestern food. He was among the first to begin searching out local suppliers, much like what Alice Waters was doing around that time at Chez Panisse in California. He just didn't get as much fanfare for doing so.

What was offered was elevated granny food, especially at first. It got a little more sophisticated later on, and it was always served elegantly. The *Post-Dispatch* critic's first visit showed a meal of tomato bouillon, cube steaks in a stroganoff-like gravy with potatoes and cauliflower and chocolate cake. That early, it was politely explained to diners that "whatever we cook is what you eat." (Perry apologized that the pear jam for the bread was not homemade.) Perry understood that midwesterners like their desserts, and soon the menu was offering choices like bourbon chiffon pie, chocolate pudding and spice cake with orange icing.

Perry ran the front of the house; originally, Jim Belshaw was the cook. Waiters did not wear tuxedos, but clean blue shirts and large waiters' aprons. The establishment added lunch and then what Perry called a Sunday farm breakfast, which causes some of us to recall a maple-glazed chicken breast as one component of the three-course menu. Grandma probably never made that. For a while, there was even a late supper offered one night a week. Nighttime entrées were mostly beef and pork with an occasional welcome appearance of chicken and dumplings. Greg Mosberger took over the kitchen for many years.

Perry received national notice for his pioneering efforts in the use of local ingredients and regional cuisine to a degree that St. Louis seemed never to realize. In 1982, he changed the name of the restaurant to his own moniker. For the first national celebration of the birthday of James Beard, a pioneer in recognizing American cuisine as distinct, the restaurant participated in the effort to buy the townhouse of the late writer in order to establish a foundation. The event charged $100 a head and featured food from Beard's recipes, including beef rolls with kumquat, Beard's mother's take on tomato soup and baked beans, veal shanks, potatoes hashed in cream, fresh asparagus and rhubarb pie with strawberry ice cream.

In 1988, the restaurant moved to a downtown hotel, and things somehow began to fall apart, with both service and food losing their spark. That lasted less than two years, and a return to the original location stayed open only a few months. Perry moved to Cincinnati and eventually returned to the St. Louis area in various capacities.

He died on Christmas Day 2017, with a surprising lack of reporting in local media.

KING LOUIE'S

One of the places most mentioned when the category of restaurants gone too soon comes up is King Louie's. There was just something about its near-universal appeal over the years that brings about a faraway look and, in extreme cases, a sigh when it's discussed. The brick building on Thirty-Ninth Street at Chouteau was the hospitality house for the Otto F. Stiefel Union Brewery, built in 1915 in a neighborhood that was at that time stockyards and slaughterhouses. In living memory, it housed the Billy Goat Hill Saloon, which got traffic from St. Louis University Hospitals and Pevely Dairy nearby. And if that name sounds familiar, the potato chips of the same name are indeed descended from those relished by beer drinkers at the saloon while they listened to local bands.

The building sat fallow for a long time. Then, in 1995, Matt McGuire, a local guy who was a graduate of the Art Institute of Chicago, and his pal Patrick Holloran, another St. Louis kid, decided to open an eatery there.

At first, it was mostly sandwiches and pizzas, although in fairly sophisticated versions thereof. The turkey club sandwich was spoken of approvingly in certain circles. There was lots of beer on tap, and cider as well, something very unusual that long ago, and a decent wine list, but still, it was hard to imagine that this was a place that would end up with *Wine Spectator* awards. It was, though, very popular despite being somewhat off the beaten path.

Around 1999, the evolution of the restaurant became evident. The bar moved into a room to the south, and an ancient tiger's-eye oak backbar gave the room gravitas. White tablecloths appeared. The wine list and the food, from the kitchen helmed by McGuire's (vegetarian) cousin Kirk Warner, flourished merrily. McGuire's favorite may have been the bouillabaisse, he says. The bread was from Black Bear, the great anarchist bakery on Cherokee Street.

And it wasn't just the food. McGuire, the front-of-house guy, hired as carefully as that other well-known St. Louis restaurateur, Danny Meyer—Meyer, of course, works in New York. These were folks who were knowledgeable, pleasant and obliging. It was the whole package for a diner's experience.

Everybody went to visit King Louie—not to pay homage, but to feel at home. Tony LaRussa, the Cardinals manager, could be found at the end of the bar after a night game, quietly having dinner and reading a book. Maestro Hans Vonk, when he helmed the St. Louis Symphony, often had lunch there on Fridays, a glass of beer and a sandwich at his booth, reading a newspaper—and giving restaurant recommendations in Amsterdam if approached politely. A local developer dining there managed to leave $1,500 in cash in an envelope on a table and got it back intact. A soon-to-depart editor of the *St. Louis Post-Dispatch* was once heard singing loudly at his table, quite out of character for the gentleman in question.

McGuire's father, the late John McGuire, wrote for the *Post-Dispatch*. He and a somewhat raffish group of other newspapermen (including my husband, a good friend of John's) and saloonkeepers, mostly retired, would meet in the bar for lunch on Fridays. The group was particularly fond of one of the bartenders, a young woman named Holly Boettigheimer, who was both very smart and very cute. At that point, Cary McDowell, now of the Pi Pizza group, was running the kitchen and appreciated the bartender as much as the older gentlemen did. More, in fact, because after a while it seemed apparent that they were considering marriage. The elders conferred. It seemed to them that if this pup were going to claim the lass they considered, in a completely avuncular sense, theirs, he should be expected to give them something in exchange for their collective blessing, a fine cow, perhaps, and a couple of fat sheep. The following Friday, McDowell barreled up to the group at the bar and reached in his pocket. "There!," he proclaimed. "Will *this* satisfy you?" And he slammed down a handful of plastic farm animals.

When Itzhak Perlman was taken to dinner post-symphony by a group of a dozen or so society types, it was a pretty stiff affair. McGuire, in fact, said, "It was like dining with the Pope." An elderly guy wearing hearing aids sat with a friend at a table nearby, regarding Perlman and the group for a while. Suddenly, he said loudly, "Hey!" Perlman turned to the guy, and responded "Yeah?", both men speaking in tones that wouldn't have been out place on the streets of New York, which is where Perlman grew up. "I saw your show last night," announced the gent. "Howja like it?" asked Perlman. There was a pause. The guy shrugged. "It was okay." Perlman's hosts gasped. Perlman, on the other hand, didn't stop laughing for the rest of the night.

The main dining room had a fireplace and two levels, but it was the bar that truly charmed. Once a patio was installed behind the barroom and big shuttered windows were added to utilize the afternoon sun, it was a deeply handsome space. (Anheuser-Busch's advertising agency took over the place one day, removed all the bottles and filmed a commercial there with August Busch IV, using the gorgeous backbar.) The patio was planted with tall grasses to block most of the view of the many railroad tracks and with lots of herbs and other plants for the kitchen's use. A wood-fired cooking area was utilized nightly. The King even had that great St. Louis necessity: parking.

Like Camelot, it was great while it lasted. But Chouteau Avenue closed for a while for construction, and then there was the massive Highway 40 closure that sent the crowds from St. Louis County in search of other roads to travel. Finally, this King breathed his last on July 7, 2007.

LETTUCE LEAF

The Lettuce Leaf was a restaurant—and then a small group of restaurants—that was before its time. Started by Bill Saigh, who taught marketing at Saint Louis University, and his wife, Christine, it was a salad restaurant. Oh, there were a few other things to eat, but it was clearly focused on salad as a main dish. Saigh got his start in the food business while he was in college, managing concessions at the old Sportsman's Park, where the St. Louis Browns and the St. Louis Cardinals baseball clubs played. His brother Fred owned the Cardinals during that time, but Bill became a university professor. When a sabbatical fell through, he and his wife decided to try opening a restaurant, something they'd been pondering for a while. Financing was difficult; he was turned down, he said, by seventeen banks until he got a loan from the Small Business Administration.

What would prove to be the first Lettuce Leaf opened a couple of doors away from the St. Louis County Courthouse in Clayton in 1976. Guests entered, and while there was a written list of the various salads, what was more important was that they walked around a refrigerated waist-high case displaying each salad, freshly made. Diners could see what they could be eating. From Saigh's standpoint, it also helped increase turnover in the restaurant. Servers could just take orders, eliminating the initial trip to offer menus and then on their return answer questions about the varieties of salads.

Some salads were classic, like the Cobb, a salad the restaurant styled the American chef, and the Caesar salad. But they were among the first to introduce the *salade Niçoise* to St. Louis. Another innovation was the taco salad, long before it became ubiquitous. Rather than a limp flour tortilla "bowl," the edge of the plate was lined with fresh tortilla chips, and the lettuce and tomato were topped with hot chili (without beans) and cheese, making for what was, in effect, a make-it-yourself nacho dish. A soup of the day was always on hand, and a few sandwiches as well, plus a hot vegetable plate with cheese sauce and a quiche. The salads and soups were always

Matchbook from the Lettuce Leaf. *Courtesy of Sally Taylor.*

accompanied by a fresh softball-sized yeast roll and real butter. Still, it was the "rabbit food" that primarily drew the crowds.

Not surprisingly, the decor featured greenery, too. The original location had a skylight to expand the light for hanging plants, along with the natural wood. One patron remembers that her idea of a fine afternoon was a salad, a carafe of wine and a book from Page One, the bookstore across the street.

Evenings proved to be as busy as lunchtime, but without a line waiting for tables. The next year, there was a location downtown. The year after that, a location opened in the Country Club Plaza district in Kansas City. More St. Louis outposts followed, including a 1980 opening in Westport Plaza, a daring second-floor site in an area unaccustomed to that sort of popularly priced eatery in such a location. In 1984, one opened at Crestwood Plaza, when the mall was newly enclosed and renamed, after being Crestwood Mall for almost three decades. Downsizing began in 1989, with Kansas City and Crestwood closing. In 1991, the Saighs sold the remaining three restaurants. The downtown space became Joseph's Cafe. The Clayton and Westport locations were combined into one site at Chesterfield Mall and closed in 2002.

LITTLE ITALY

Mario Bruno was a man who always seemed to enjoy his work. A chef from Cosenza, Italy, a city in Calabria south of Naples, he came to St. Louis in 1966 to join aunts and an uncle who were already here. On one of his trips home, he met and married another chef, Giovanna. In 1978, they opened Little Italy on Hampton Avenue.

It really was little, at least at first, seating around thirty-five, with lots of pasta as well as the expected riffs on things like veal and chicken breast. Their cheesecake was "highly recommended," according to the *Post-Dispatch* reviewer, but there were only five kinds of wine.

The latter problem didn't last very long, apparently. Within three years, the wine list had been wildly expanded, thanks to the always enthusiastic Mario. A

New Orleans food writer, on meeting a St. Louisan, remarked that, at a huge wine tasting, he'd met "some Bruno guy from St. Louis, who really knew his stuff." The *Post-Dispatch* critic, in a new review, now was calling the wine list "a joy." He also remarked on the prevalence of garlic in the first of his two meals for that review and then relayed an overheard scenario. On the night of the heavy garlic, Bruno stopped to visit with one nearby diner and then went on to take an order at another table. He asked the first how she was enjoying her meal. "Everything was wonderful," said the woman. "But it might have been better with more garlic." At the next table, the diner ordered a steak. "And don't forget to chop some extra garlic on top," he added.

Giovanna ruled the kitchen, and the ebullient Mario handled the front of the house, including the wine cellar, in a reversal of the common European style. There was also another waitress, but that was it for a number of years, even after they expanded into the next storefront, bringing their total seating to fifty or so.

Mario, though, later admitted that he never liked the location. Six years after the opening, he quietly bought a new building on Southwest Avenue just east of Hampton, much closer to The Hill, St. Louis's traditional Italian neighborhood. That was 1984. For five years, he served as his own general contractor as well as being in the restaurant at night.

The move to the new location occurred in 1989. He added his family name onto that of the restaurant, and it became Bruno's Little Italy. Stained-glass windows, paintings from an artist friend in Italy, two dining rooms—one solely for nonsmokers—plus a bar marked the new location. The capacity was up to seventy, and Giovanna still ran the kitchen. Soon, one of their daughters, Paula, could be seen shadowing her father and the servers as they worked, and then the second, Nadia, followed.

There was a shadow on the horizon, though. Mario's kidneys were failing. In 1992, he had a kidney transplant. The women in his family kept the restaurant going through that. Two years later, however, in the autumn of 1994, he passed away. Giovanna and her daughters continued to run Bruno's Little Italy until its closing in 1998.

LT. ROBERT E. LEE

St. Louis has a love-hate relationship with the Mississippi River. It's like an elderly relative who's got a little money but is intermittently very unpleasant to be around. And, keeping that theme, it's a relative we acknowledge we're kin to, but how often do we ever actually pay her much attention? Besides, it's hard to figure out where to park near where she lives, always a concern for St. Louisans.

To some degree, that's an explanation for the story of the Lt. Robert E. Lee, the floating restaurant. (Lee, of course, was the head of the Confederate army, but as a young lieutenant he served at Jefferson Barracks, south of downtown St. Louis, and helped map the Mississippi River.) It was definitely not the historic steamboat that raced the *Natchez* in 1870. This *Lee* was built in Greenville, Mississippi, on an existing hull originally crafted for the U.S. Army Corps of Engineers and brought to the riverfront in 1969.

Docked on the levee—technically Leonor K. Sullivan Boulevard, named for the first female member of the U.S. Congress from Missouri—the restaurant was not an excursion boat, a fact that always confused patrons and would-be patrons. The only movement was the rise and fall of the boat with the river levels.

At least that was the way it was supposed to be. Looking back, the boat was star-crossed, but it certainly wasn't because it was too small or not attractive enough. Four decks held six dining rooms, one of which seated 275. The decor evoked a fine Victorian parlor, minus the immense plants. Large windows allowed for admiring the river. The food was steaks, seafood and a definite New Orleans influence, with things like gumbo and bread pudding making their way onto the menu. For a while, one deck was for seafood and another for steaks. For a number of years, one room was a dinner theater with a group called the Natchez River Review singing and serving. The lower-level saloon had ragtime and Dixieland jazz, with local musicians like Singleton Palmer and Muggsy Sprecher. "If you have never heard 'Ragtime Cowboy Joe' played on a tuba, you are missing an experience," remarked Dick Richmond, the entertainment reporter for the *Post-Dispatch*.

Besides the dinner theater and the sheer experience of eating on the water, there was other drama. In 1976, a runaway grain barge struck the restaurant. No one was hurt, but an electrical cable snapped, starting a small fire. The boat, of course, was evacuated, although one patron refused to leave the dining room until she finished her drink. A few days later, a sign appeared over the gangway: "Barge In On Us Today."

In hindsight, we forget how badly the Mississippi flooded in 1983. That's not a misprint; the Big One of '93 was yet to come. There had been another flood in December 1982, but this April/May event was, when it happened, the third worst of the century. The most spectacular consequence was on the

Menu cover from Lt. Robert E. Lee. *Courtesy of Missouri Historical Society.*

evening of April 3, 1983, when barges loaded with crude oil crashed into the Poplar Street Bridge. Two of them exploded. One eyewitness reported that the explosion was higher than the Arch. Another hit barges moored at a Monsanto plant on the Illinois side of the river. The escaping oil floating on the river caught fire and began to flow downstream. In the restaurant, people could feel the heat and see the flames. No damage was done, however, to any of the boats moored on the levee.

The flood at that point had only just begun; the high water lasted almost a month. A skeleton crew of employees had gotten to the restaurant in December by rowboat, but this time there was too much water from heavy spring rains and fast-melting winter snows to do even that.

The Flood of 1993 was yet to come. But the boat went through a series of owners, with corporations buying it, undergoing mergers and selling it, and then individuals getting in on things, including John Connelly, the man who bought the much-loved *Admiral* excursion ship and hoped to turn it into a gambling boat. Every move was a little more destabilizing.

After the five-hundred-year flood of 1993, the boat closed and was dormant for a while. By 1995, it was up for sale again without reopening. In 2001, it operated briefly as Mesquite Charlie's, and by 2003, it had become Yackey's on the River. In 2004, it was towed to Kimmswick—it never had engines or a rudder—and didn't work as a restaurant there, either. Within two years, it was towed back to St. Louis.

It burned to the waterline at a repair yard just north of downtown, a spectacular end, in 2010. The origin of the fire was apparently never determined. A new owner was going to move it to St. Charles. Perhaps the boat was tired of traveling.

MAJESTIC RESTAURANT

What percentage of customers of the Majestic Restaurant never had any meal other than breakfast there? Surely, it must have been more than half, even though the restaurant served dinner until relatively late, especially after it expanded next door and put in a bar. The Majestic—like any old friend, it was only referred to by its first name—was, in effect, a diner, a quiet neighborhood restaurant whose neighborhood changed around it.

When it opened in 1957, it was Jimmy's Majestic Restaurant, owned by Jimmy Speropoulos. Four years later, Lou Politis, who worked there, purchased it from his employer and soon brought his brother Bill into the business. It remained in the family through the next generation, with Lou's son Pete and Bill's son Alex helping to run things until its closure in 2015.

The intersection of Laclede Avenue and Euclid was never totally somnolent, even before the urban awakening of the Central West End. Martin's Variety Store was a few doors east of the intersection; a small grocery store and a couple of bars quietly stayed in business. Kean's

Really Golden Oldies

Interior of the Majestic Restaurant. *Courtesy of Student Life.*

Drug at the northwest corner was seemingly the anchor, with pharmacists Bernard and David Kean and the ever-youthful Art Perry running things. The Majestic was at the southwest corner, the sort of place that nursing students from the three schools of nursing in the area, the pharmacy students and even the lordly medical students would go when they could scrape together a few shekels and escape dormitory or hospital food. Things began to heat up in the 1970s, of course, and that meant more people discovered the modest little place with reasonably priced traditional American food and a few Greek specialties.

It was, even through the uptick in the area, very neighborhood-y, especially on weekdays. Pete Politis tells tales of the first landing of the space shuttle *Columbia* in 1981, when everyone left their food and went into the bar to watch the event. A few months after that, the huge snow that walloped St. Louis one Saturday didn't stop the Majestic from opening. Pete commandeered a Jeep, picked up his employees and plowed through the white stuff. The place, he reported, was jammed all day. On the other hand, a *Post-Dispatch* columnist was on hand to watch federal marshals serve papers on a fellow who hadn't paid his parking tickets in the city of St. Louis.

In 1987, a little shudder of fear ran through the regulars. The lease, the rumor had it, was up, and there was a question about it being signed or not. But, no, things continued as before, and the coffee flowed. That breakfast menu that fed so many folks? Beyond the usual stuff, there were choices like silver-dollar blues, small blueberry pancakes (fat but tender) and the Bill's Special omelet, with gyro meat, feta cheese, tomato and onion. (Did we mention the owners were Greek?) And just to prove it really was in St. Louis and not in, say, Queens, brains and eggs were on the menu. The bar picked up some steam and occasionally had Greek music after the nearby Grecian Gardens closed.

Eventually, the decision was made by the Politis family to close things down, and in the spring of 2015, they sliced their last gyro.

MEDART'S

No one looking at the south side of Clayton Road a few hundred feet west of where Skinker Boulevard turns into McCausland Avenue would be surprised to see the half-timbered buildings there. The sign proclaims Cheshire Inn, so British-sounding. But those buildings, except for the newer hotel, were originally Medart's, or at times, Bill Medart's. The scion of a local manufacturing family, Bill had met and married a Hollywood actress named Blossom Breneman who was originally from Kirkwood. But as the economy began to go in the tank with the Depression, he decided the hamburger—a sandwich whose glories were being discovered by more people—was what he'd sell folks. The couple returned to St. Louis to open a restaurant.

The original building was opened in 1930 or 1931 as a hamburger stand and was an immediate hit. At first, Bill ran the grill and Blossom made coconut pies. A second location came in 1933 on South Kingshighway, now the site of Uncle Bill's Pancake House. Expansion at the original site began in 1934 with a large, elegant addition with more half-timbering. Called the Olde Cheshire, it, too, thrived as the menu became more elaborate. Amazingly, despite the financial problems across the country, Bill expanded again in 1939, the largest addition of all, and a final one in 1943, this building known as the Rose and Crown.

What did they feed the crowds that obviously came? Menus from the 1930s feature some unusual descriptions for a couple of standards. A "hamburger au gratin" was obviously their description of a cheeseburger, never mind that *au gratin* really doesn't mean "with cheese." (*Gratin* refers to a top crust on a dish that comes from baking or broiling.) The burgers arrived partly wrapped to contain the juices that always dripped off, and their special sauce. What was it? Arguments continue on that, but it seems to have been a Thousand Island–style dressing, chunky with bits of pickle and onion in a mayo base with some horseradish thrown in.

A "molten cheese sandwich" was also offered—easy to figure out. But on that same menu comes what seems to be a very early—perhaps the first appearance—of a very local and not widely known sandwich, the Saint Paul. A Saint Paul consists of an egg foo yong patty with lettuce, tomato and mayonnaise on white bread. These days, it can be found at carryout Chinese restaurants.

By the 1940s, with the more elaborate dining rooms came more elaborate food. By the end of the decade, the menu offered seven different curries and had a section titled "chafing dishes," including exotica like chicken livers with mushrooms and squab with seedless grapes and white wine. Things obviously rocked—it was open until 4:00 a.m. on Saturday nights, long after the bars had closed. A contemporary description says it was big with college students and after-theater diners.

It wasn't all easy times. A bitter nine-month strike with the Waitress Union was marked with fistfights. Medart, the publisher of the *Labor Tribune* and the leader of the Bartenders Union had at it, resulting in arrests and a fractured bone in a policeman helping out, before the strike ended in the spring of 1942. Medart died in 1951, plunging from the balcony of a hotel in Paris that faced the Tuileries Gardens, the death ruled a suicide. Blossom married again, to a man named Maurice Amara. Together, they kept the restaurant until it was sold to Stephen J. Apted of the restaurant family that began with Miss Hulling's, and he turned it into the Cheshire Inn.

MISS HULLING'S

There was a time a few decades back when the words *Miss Hulling's* would evoke many different thoughts, including different locations. Florence Hulling came to St. Louis as a young woman from her home in Mascoutah, Illinois, thinking she would like to be a telephone operator. She didn't get hired and took a job in a private home as a housekeeper and cook. After a year, she went to work at Childs Restaurant, one of the very first restaurant chains in the United States, known for their extreme cleanliness and the signature butter cakes they cooked on griddles in their front window. (Butter cakes were neither pancakes nor pastries, but a yeast-raised round of dough vaguely like an English muffin. It was served hot with butter melting on top and a bit of syrup.)

Florence became a manager at Childs. She saved her money and, by 1928—or 1929 or 1930; accounts vary—had accumulated $600. She took a deep breath and plunged her life's savings into rent for a restaurant in the basement of the Hotel Missouri on Locust Street. It was a brave move as the Depression roared on, but, she said years later, the "suppliers were wonderful to me," not expecting payment immediately. Many of the personnel from Childs, which was reeling not only from the economy but also from one of the next generation of owners' decision to go vegetarian, happily moved over to work for Miss Florence Hulling.

In 1931, she married a customer, Stephen R. Apted, who began to run the business end of things. Two years later, their only child, Stephen J., was born. He, too, would go into the family business. The following year, 1934, they moved Miss Hulling's across the street to the northwest corner of Locust and Eleventh Streets, the location most of us remember.

Having Stephen Apted tending to the business end of things freed up Miss Florence, as she was known in the restaurant, to focus on what was happening in the establishment. As an employer, she had high standards. One longtime employee said that when she was wiping down a table, Miss Florence said, no, have a cloth in each hand to wipe. Years later, the employee was running the cafeteria line. Employees, if they met her standards, did tend to stay a long time. But it was all firmly organized, including a starting bell as each day began and as customers were about to walk in.

Being so close to Twelfth Street, now Tucker Boulevard, meant that diners weren't just the downtown office workers and shoppers who'd come down to the three major department stores: Scruggs, Vandervoort and Barney; Famous-Barr; and Stix, Baer and Fuller. It drew the courthouse crowd, too. One small room every Thursday held the informal group referred to as the "lawyers' roundtable." Sometimes, an unwitting newcomer would be asked to move by some regular because the newbie was sitting in a spot the regular considered his.

At first, it was "grandma food"—traditional American dishes that were not exotic—and those dishes were always present on the line, certainly. There was meatloaf and mashed potatoes, liver and onions, baked whitefish with creole sauce and a casserole called sour cream noodle bake, its recipe passed on for home cooks. The carrot and marshmallow salad was a popular favorite, and so was the much-loved creamed spinach.

The spinach became party to an anecdote. A young man had applied for a job as a sportswriter at the *St. Louis Post-Dispatch*. They liked his previous work well enough to bring him and his wife down from Iowa for an interview. The legendary sports editor J. Roy Stockton took the young couple to lunch at Miss Hulling's. "Get the creamed spinach," advised Stockton, turning to the young man, who was of below-average height. "It'll make you grow."

Really Golden Oldies

FEATURES
HAWKS HOME GAME SPECIAL
Before every game—10 ounce Sirloin Steak Dinner @ $3.00
Includes Salad, Hot Rolls with Butter, Potato, Beverage
TABLE SERVICE
or
CAFETERIA

Top: Pregame dinner special, undated. The Hawks played in St. Louis from 1955 to 1968. *Courtesy Donald M. Casalone.*

Left: Cookbook cover, 1969. *Courtesy St. Louis Public Library.*

They hired the sportswriter, who went on to a long and honored career. But even Miss Hulling's creamed spinach didn't make him any taller.

After a while, the offerings expanded to include more sophisticated dishes, but the standards were irreplaceable. And they were always the same. No one tinkered with recipes. It was important that they be consistent. Some patrons ate there every day, even twice a day; no alteration would go unnoticed. Miss Florence even published a cookbook.

At two stories, with a capacity of 550 people, the restaurant grew eventually to have a bakery and a takeout counter. The pink walls seemed the perfect setting for white boxes neatly tied with string. Best of all, perhaps, was that the boxes often held the house's signature dessert, split cake. Originally available in lemon and chocolate, the loaves were five layers of tender yellow cake, each sandwiched with either a lemon or chocolate filling and frosted with a white lemon or dark chocolate icing.

As the younger Steve Apted entered the business, he began to branch out. They bought Medart's, another old St. Louis restaurant. He said the first guest after the purchase asked for his mother's chicken pot pie. Other places not bearing the Hulling's name began. There had briefly been a satellite operation downtown, but it didn't remain. They did food service at some local hospitals. I can personally attest that on a midnight shift in an ICU, the idea of a piece of split lemon cake around 4:00 a.m. is a fine thing.

Downtown began to sag, though, and in 1993, Miss Hulling's and the sit-down restaurant and bar that adjoined it and that were part of the restaurant group all closed. The bakery stayed open, but only for a while.

One happy remnant survives to this day. The split cakes are thriving, identical to their ancestors, and being sold at Straub's, the local grocer. The store reports that they remain immensely popular and are even shipped to nostalgic ex–St. Louisans.

NANTUCKET COVE

People remember restaurants for the darnedest reasons. For many, Nantucket Cove was the site of romantic dates, even proposals. But for some of us, it was where we first tackled a whole lobster.

Tucked into the West Pine side of the Forest Park–facing Frontenac Apartments, it opened in 1959. There were valets to take automobiles, a small bridge to cross and then an entrance into a suite of rooms that surely didn't feel like the Midwest. It was dark and romantic and nautical, with some rough boards from old barns (in the Ozarks, it turned out), ships' lanterns and all kinds of antiques. The smallest dining room, called the Revere Room, sported a lantern that was said to have been made by Paul Revere. Several other items in the room, including furniture, dated to the nineteenth century. All of it was decorative, of course; the regular captain's chairs were more comfortable than the ancient straight-backed ones.

The restaurant was the creation of Gordon Heiss, the president of the Mayfair-Lenox group of hotels. Its decor was done by a St. Louisan named Abe Rovak. Nantucket, as it was referred to, brought in seafood by air freight and at one point was practically the only place in town to get fresh oysters year-round. There were, of course, freshwater choices available, but it was the seafood, and particularly the lobster, that made the restaurant's reputation. Had anyone seen lobster bibs in town before this?

On entering, there was a bar and the trickling water of the lobster pound and trout run. The larger dining room had a slightly elevated area

Interior of Nantucket Cove. *Courtesy of Missouri Historical Society.*

with a rail known as the upper deck, providing a pleasant view of the other diners digging in. It was allegedly an informal restaurant, and certainly men appeared without ties, but it's hard to imagine anyone showed up in shorts and T-shirts. It was definitely date-night material and suitable for business dinners.

In reminiscing, people mention several specific things. The lobsters, of course, which seemed always to be perfectly cooked. The usual method was steaming, and that appears to have been the most popular, although there were more elaborate preparations for the crustacean. The attacking of the lobster occasionally had an unwitting side effect; at least one former patron reports having a piece of bright red shell land on his sport coat as some diner nearby had a little too much mojo on the prying. No melted butter apparently made the flight.

The signature recipe of the house, though, was the Mayfair salad dressing, which Heiss had, of course, brought from the Mayfair Hotel, for which it was named. A creamy, rich dressing, its allure, probably unknown to most of the people who ate it, was due to plenty of anchovies. The recipe was a carefully guarded secret, although several versions are still served here in St. Louis. The bar also did a killer brandy Alexander, thick and slushy with ice. It made for some memorable meals.

Heiss franchised the concept around 1967, and there were branches in Chicago and Kansas City. In 1968, they were sold to Frank and Charlie Potts, who had been involved in their management. In 1972, the Potts family purchased the location here. There was also an interesting connection to Barnes Hospital, five blocks south. Queeny Tower, at the southwestern corner of the block that Barnes occupied, was something very different in a hospital complex. The tower contained the hospital pharmacy, a lobby, physician offices and patient floors—and then hotel rooms and, on the top floor, a restaurant. (The roof had a swimming pool.) Heiss and then Potts ran the Queeny Tower Restaurant, whose decor was also done by Abe Rovak. More than one employee, tired of cafeteria food, went up for a Mayfair salad, and I speak from personal experience.

The restaurant moved to Clayton in the autumn of 1994, at the corner of Hanley and Carondelet. The site had previously housed Dierdorf and Hart's Steakhouse and Bernard Douteau's Giarrosto. A year later, it was sold to Amer Hawatmeh, and it closed in 1999.

The Mayfair dressing recipe is in our recipe section.

NAUGLES TACOS AND BURGERS

Is there any sense in talking about a chain restaurant in a book like this? Considering the way St. Louis felt about Naugles, the answer would be a resounding "yes." Properly titled Naugles Tacos and Burgers, the California-based chain arrived here in the mid-to-late 1970s. By the end of 1983, there would be twenty locations.

There must have been people who ate in the restaurants (emphasis on *in*), and there were indeed booths and tables, but the action was in the drive-through. Originally, all locations were open twenty-four hours a day, one of the rules of Dick Naugle, the founder. While St. Louis stayed up surprisingly late in the fifties and even the early sixties, to judge from restaurant ads of the period, by the time Naugles came to town, we were catching up on our sleep, so an all-night place had a ready audience.

One of those sites was on McCausland Avenue just south of the Hi-Pointe Theatre, barely within the city limits. Late at night, particularly on weekends, the line waiting at the drive-through went out of the lot and north up McCausland. Particularly when there had been something going on at the Checkerdome, formerly the St. Louis Arena, Naugles was slammed. It was a little less maniacal after baseball games.

Opening somewhat later was the former Phillips 66 service station on South Grand Boulevard, often referred to as "the flying saucer building" because of its large circular roof. It's directly across the street from St. Louis University's Reinert Hall, which has a history of its own, since it was built as a Ramada Inn. The student population immediately understood the importance of the arrival of Naugles in the neighborhood.

It was definitely popular with the young and young-at-heart, but there were times when things got somewhat out of hand. The neighbors of the McCausland store were concerned about trash, traffic, groups talking loudly and other results of too much beer. Their then-alderman Dan McGuire seemed to be perpetually working on the problem, with mixed results. At one point, he introduced a bill proposing that businesses within one hundred feet of a dwelling close from 10:00 p.m. until 6:00 a.m. The bill never passed, and not just because the residents discovered that Wendy's wanted to open right across the street from Naugles. (That never came to pass, either.)

The hamburgers were actually pretty good, but not nearly as popular as the Mexican food. Crossroads School, in the Central West End, sent out for Naugles for the kids every Thursday for a while as part of a weekly rotation of local restaurants, the result of an effort to contribute to the local economy and the idea that getting adolescents to actually eat at school was important to learning. (The school also had cooking classes.)

Certainly Naugles was the first fast-food place in town to offer Mexican breakfast foods—possibly the first one, period. Things were cooked from scratch; one employee talks about going through fifty-pound bags of pinto beans to make sure there were no rocks in the legumes. Burritos were almost as big as a forearm but very tricky to eat while driving, the filling sliding languorously out the back end unless careful attention was paid. The result landed on the driver, or on the steering wheel.

What happened to Naugles? Was the expansion too fast? It was in deep trouble by 1985, losing money like mad. It had never advertised, relying instead on word of mouth. Some people said part of the problem was that the name didn't tell the unknowing passerby what the place sold; "tacos and burgers" was in small print, if on signs at all. Stores closed, and the chain was sold to Del Taco. It was said that the last four locations to change their identities to Del Taco were the remaining St. Louis ones.

In recent years, there was an effort to resurrect the name and the concept, but it doesn't seem to have gone anywhere. When the attempt at resurrection was still being talked up, the revivers said they were particularly looking at the rabid fan bases in Riverside, California; Las Vegas, Nevada; and St. Louis.

We'd be glad to have them back.

NOAH'S ARK

There's an old line from the ineffable W.C. Fields: "It was a woman who drove me to drink, and I never had the courtesy to thank her." Noah's Ark, the unforgettable-looking restaurant on I-70 in St. Charles, introduced the area to clam chowder, and I suppose we never thanked the restaurant, either.

Certainly Howard Johnson's was ladling the creamy soup before that, but the chowder at the Ark just seemed to wake St. Louis up to how tasty it was. Actually, we should have thanked David Flavan, an airline pilot, and his brother John, a buyer for Lammert's Furniture. The men came up with the Noah's Ark concept and then brought it to life.

Would you believe it was originally going to be a steamship? Indeed, it was, with a farmyard of animals outside. But health regulations didn't allow live animals within a specified distance of a restaurant, so that was the end of that. Fiberglass animals, David Flavan later said, seemed to be the answer.

But would they get carried off by pranksters? Does the sun rise in the east? The solution, they decided, was to put them on the roof. And so the idea of the ark came to be. It opened in 1968.

We all loved that clam chowder so much that by 1972 they were making four hundred to five hundred gallons a week, arriving as an individual serving or as a crock for the table. There was a lunch buffet, and a lot of business traffic for that. The salad bar at night was immense. Many people still think of it as a place where they had dates or went on the night of their prom. A few have even held onto the orange plastic giraffe cocktail stirrers from the Ark; the picks for cocktail garnishes like orange slices or martini olives were also giraffes, albeit shorter ones. They looked like children's toys from a cereal box, but surely the customers weren't young ones if they were having an alcoholic beverage.

By 1979, dinner theater was attempted in the Animal Kingdom Room. In 1982, a late-night fire damaged part of the restaurant, and an employee was charged with arson. Within a few days, it reopened, although the dining room remained unusable for a while. The Animal Kingdom Room and the Cage Room were used instead.

In 1992, the Ark was leased out and became Captain Tony's, which also functioned as a dance club. Rent disputes followed; it finally closed altogether in 2000. Before it was demolished, the blog Underground Ozarks went into the building in 2006, documenting what it looked like, which was pretty sad.

The demolition took place in 2007.

PARKMOOR

It all began with a tray. For the increasingly large number of people who don't remember drive-in restaurants, food often arrived on a tray that could be hung on the driver's window. The window had to be open to hold the tray, so it was great in decent weather, but miserable, of course, in the cold or rain. Nevertheless, it was an improvement in the days before cars had cupholders. The tray was invented by William L McGinley in 1930. He was a Texan who went on the road to sell his tray to the burgeoning drive-in business, but he struck out in St. Louis. There were simply no drive-ins in town. At some point, the light bulb went on; in 1931, he moved his family to St. Louis and opened one himself. It was a brave move in the early years of the Depression.

Menu cover from Parkmoor, early 1950s, showing locations. *Courtesy of Missouri Historical Society.*

Really Golden Oldies

Illustration from Parkmoor menu cover, by Vic Vac. *Courtesy of Missouri Historical Society.*

Named the Parkmoor, it was at Clayton Road and Big Bend Boulevard, near Washington University, Christian Brothers College prep school and St. Mary's Hospital. It was an immediate success, and the following year, another Parkmoor opened on North Kingshighway, near DePaul Hospital and McBride High School. A third arrived on South Kingshighway at Chippewa. In 1936, another was added at DeBaliviere and Pershing. By this time, the restaurant was known as a good place to work, and one family member would recruit another, even coming in from small towns in Missouri and Illinois.

After World War II, a Chippewa and Watson location was opened in 1950, small enough that there were no tables, only a counter, but it was the first to have speakers at each parking spot for patrons to use to place their order. Another, the largest of all with eighty parking spots and a large dining room, came to Lindbergh and Manchester in 1956. All of the locations eventually had indoor seating and plenty of the company's signature orange color. Briefly, there was a Parkmoor in Indianapolis that opened in 1940, but it closed in 1953. Others across the country with the same name were not related.

What were the crowds eating? Ice cream aplenty, made in-house, especially when it came with cake and hot fudge. Sandwiches were popular, particularly the signature big-for-its-day hamburger. Eventually known as Kingburgers, the two patties, cheese, tomato, pickle and slaw became a feature of the kitchen. Some still bemoan the loss of a hot dog topped with cheese, bacon and relish, all in a style of bun with a split top, a configuration not often seen in this part of the United States. Everyone agrees, however, that the onion rings, huge and flaky, almost like tempura, were the most remarkable thing on the menu. For a while, breakfast was offered, and there were salads and lunch or dinner entrées like fried chicken and "chop't" (their spelling) steak.

The drive-through didn't kill things, but it certainly was an accessory to murder. The South Kingshighway location was the first to close, in 1956. Despite its location across from the city's hottest Top 40 radio station, KXOK (there's no indication that the proximity of the Parkmoor caused KXOK to locate near hamburgers), the North Kingshighway site closed in 1967. Another interesting neighborhood had arisen around the DeBaliviere location, full of clubs, fancier restaurants and an art movie house, but that didn't help; it closed in 1969, along with the Chippewa store. In 1970, the Parkmoor at Lindbergh and Manchester shuttered; it's now part of an automobile dealership.

But the family kept the Clayton–Big Bend location, razed the early buildings, ended curb service and built a modern Googie-style building, the sort that epitomized the space-age sort of feeling. They kept the orange, of course, and as many loyal employees as they could. The new building at the original location opened in 1969 with 165 seats.

In 1977, William McGinley, living in Dallas and mainly running the tray company, had a stroke; he passed away in 1980. His daughter Lou Ellen took over the businesses when her father became ill. But the national chain restaurants' popularity took their toll, and in 1999, the last Parkmoor closed.

The chain's popularity can be judged by the fact that the Parkmoor is far and away the restaurant people urged me to write about most when they learned I was writing this book.

The Parkmoor Chickburger is featured in the recipe chapter.

PELICAN'S CAFE

Why resist the urge to begin discussing Pelican's Cafe with the opening of this limerick?

A wonderful bird is the pelican.
His beak can hold more than his belly can.

Surprisingly, it's not from Ogden Nash but a newspaperman named Dixon Lanier Merritt. Merritt, who died in 1971, surely could have eaten at Pelican's Cafe before it closed.

Located at the northeast corner of South Grand and Shenandoah in a building that has been given landmark status by the City of St. Louis, it's one of only three restaurant sites that hold the status. The others are Bevo Mill and Al Smith's/the Feasting Fox. What all three have in common is that their roots come from the brewery business.

Unlike the other two, Pelican's did not spring from Anheuser-Busch roots. It was built by brewer Anton Griesedieck in 1895. Griesedieck hired Carl Anscheutz to run it, and it was known as Anscheutz' Restaurant. Carl surely knew what he was doing. He had been the general manager at Tony Faust's famous restaurant. It appears that, at some point, he bought it outright. Things must have gone well, because in 1911, he purchased a beer garden nearby, a few blocks south at South Grand and Magnolia. He changed the name of that establishment to the Mission Inn and over the next few years sank a great deal of money into renovations there. Prohibition loomed on the horizon, and it was a poor time to put capital into liquor establishments. He sold the Grand and Shenandoah property in 1925 to Demetrios James Pelican and his wife, Katharine. The Mission Inn stayed afloat for another ten years, hosting, among others, a flock of politicians. Meanwhile, Pelican's Cafe came into being.

The Pelicans were big on seafood, at one time serving 10 different kinds, including lobster. The accompanying photo was taken in the mid-1930s. It's easy to see that the beer garden that had been part of the original restaurant is still there, on the left side of the photo. Refrigeration had been around for decades, but air-conditioning? Not so common. Note the sign announcing the seventy-five-cent price of lobster.

The Pelicans sold the restaurant, but not the building, to the Laskaris family in 1956. By the time of the sale, the signature dish had been established: turtle soup. Chris Laskaris, son of the new owners, says he began working at

Pelican Cafe, mid-1930s. *Courtesy of Chris Laskaris.*

the restaurant at the age of three. The big seller in his memory was steaks; lobster wasn't as big a deal back then.

But it was a wide-ranging menu. In 1969, *Post-Dispatch* writer Ron Powers described it as "bewilderingly varied," pointing out that besides the regular menu, a mimeographed sheet offered an additional thirty-three entrées. Powers, who went on to win a Pulitzer Prize at the *Chicago Sun-Times*, laughingly acknowledges he was no restaurant critic. (The Pulitzer was for his television criticism.) Nevertheless, it's an amusing read, including noting that all the waitresses must have seen at least one Thelma Ritter movie and describing one regular who sat at his table with a portable radio on. The lightly breaded onion rings flew out of the kitchen, and the fried shrimp was treated with the same respect. Mrs. Laskaris made the baklava on the dessert menu herself.

The decor remained deeply reminiscent of the 1930s, with a big mural of underwater life a notable feature. As another newspaper story noted, "at Pelican's, it appeared eternally obvious that the best baseball player in

America was Ducky Medwick." That timelessness was one of the reasons for the cafe's charm.

In 1975, the Laskaris family decided to vacate the restaurant because of a dispute with the owners of the building, the Pelicans. It stood empty for five years and was reopened by Saleem Hanna, who owned a Middle Eastern restaurant farther south on Grand. The attempt to integrate the cuisines did not go well, and in 1982, Hanna sold the building to Robert Conway and a group of investors. They reopened it as the Pelican Cafe, but financial difficulties became overwhelming. Sadly, Conway, according to police reports, set a fire on the first floor and then committed suicide. The interior was heavily damaged.

The neon signs that were so much a part of the building have met with various fates. The curved one above the door at the corner with a pelican on it is gone completely. The tall one with the other pelican was taken apart and finally moved to two different locations. Antique Warehouse's Greg R. Rhomberg has them both and hopes to restore the sign, something he's been able to do with other treasures. The third sign, which read "Seafood" above a brilliant scarlet lobster, has been brought back to life and is in working order.

At this writing, there is discussion of a Domino's Pizza going in the building. It just won't be the same, though

PONTICELLO'S RESTAURANT

Was it the best pizza ever? And the best fried chicken? And the best onion rings? The last Ponticello's closed in 2013, and the fans still insist the answers to those questions are all an emphatic "yes."

There were several locations of Ponticello's run by various family members, starting with two brothers named Ponticello who were married to two women named Rose. Vito was a tailor, but he'd also worked at Rose's Restaurant, not named for his wife, downtown. In 1954, he and his Rose decided to open a restaurant at Goodfellow and McLaran. Angelo, the younger of the brothers, and his wife joined them. Soon, the two couples decided that four owners were too many. Vito and his wife moved to a location on Bellefontaine Road in Spanish Lake, into what they later described as "a German settlement." It's hard to know if the remark on the website, "Most folks in the area had no idea what pizza was, much less mostaccioli," is tongue in cheek or not, but surely by the sixties St. Louis was not unfamiliar with pizza. (Mostaccioli had apparently not yet become a standard dish at local wedding receptions, where it's still referred to as "muskacholli.") The building was fifty years old when they bought it, but it stayed the course with some improvements and enlarging.

Angelo and Rose added another location in Normandy on Natural Bridge, and then a third brother, Frank, decided to jump in. He opened restaurants on Chambers Road and on Airport Road. Vito, the original guy who had moved to Spanish Lake, added another location farther south on Bellefontaine at I-270 and a third in a now-defunct Ramada Inn on Dunn Road.

It was certainly St. Louis–style pizza, and many people nostalgically remark on Ponticello's being the first place they ate shrimp on a pizza. The restaurant made its own Italian sausage, grinding pork butts and seasoning it right there in the kitchen. There was live music in the bar, where, in those laid-back days, parents might have a cocktail and the youngsters, at least those old enough to be trusted alone, would have a table in the dining room for their pizza, onion rings and soda and feel very worldly indeed.

Vito and Rose's daughter Vicki and her husband, Ludwig Reiss, took over the Bellefontaine spot. The other locations closed gradually, and the Bellefontaine location baked its last pizza in 2013.

RIDDLE'S PENULTIMATE

Located across from the Tivoli Theatre in the Delmar Loop, Riddle's Penultimate was totally, deeply casual, as befitted its proximity to a university. Two rooms, the front with a bar and a very low stage against the front window on the east side of the door, and a dining room to the rear, made up the house. Low-key artwork decorated the walls, from antique St. Louis lithographs to original contemporary work to particularly significant wine posters. The music seemed just as varied, from bluegrass to pop.

While the music was fun, it was the food and drink that drew people in, whether it was before or after a movie, on a date night or just hanging out. I clearly recall a middle-aged bride quietly eating her wedding supper at one end of the bar on a Sunday evening. Alone. Her new husband was a patient in a local hospital, and after going through with the momentous ceremony, she thought the shiitake mushrooms sauteed in butter and garlic were just the thing to cap off the day's events.

The kitchen, thanks to owner-chef Andy Ayers, gloried in local ingredients before it was fashionable or even easy to get them. From something as simple as the first tomatoes of the season to persuading a local farmer selling spinach at Soulard Market not to plow under his excess (planted because he was never sure about the year's yield), to tracking down local meats, the idea took off and exploded. The results on the plate were nearly always worthwhile. Soups were splendid, like a sausage-and-succotash. Sides were never humdrum, no catchall "vegetable medleys." While there were some constants on the menu, like chicken Major Grey with chutney and sour cream, things changed so constantly that Riddle's was the first in town to print new menus every day, and it was the first restaurant to put them on its website daily.

Paula Ayers, sometimes referred to as the Dessert Queen, baked superb pies. Hot fudge sauce was made in-house. When it came to ice cream, here, too, they led the way with an aging ice-cream churn held together by Andy's uncle with homegrown engineering magic and an ability to scrounge parts. Black raspberry chocolate chip, anyone?

Service could be erratic. Andy and Paula, socially progressive, sometimes hired young ones who needed a job rather than experienced servers, but regular customers knew that going in.

It's hard to imagine that a place this free-form would have a wine list good enough to win *Wine Spectator* awards. But it did, with a wine list so big it was in a loose-leaf notebook. Lots of Missouri wine appeared on the list as well; Andy had fallen in love with it early in his career. A wide variety of beer was offered, as well as an annual beer dinner.

There was an increasing selection of European wines, too, especially French wine, as Ayers's palate grew. In 1995, French president Jacques Chirac announced that he would resume nuclear testing in the South Pacific. In Australia and in much of Europe, boycotting of French products began, including wine. Not Andy. He was opposed to nuclear testing, but he saw no reason to penalize French winemakers for their government's actions. So he announced that he was giving 10 percent of the proceeds of any French wine he sold to Greenpeace. The environmental action group's ship had actually been bombed by French agents while in harbor in New Zealand. His French wine sales more than doubled.

There was no television in the bar; Andy could be identified by his Cardinals cap but preferred radio for his baseball. The 1994 baseball season was shortened by a players' strike. Anheuser-Busch—simply "the brewery," as it's known in St. Louis—owned the team, and it began pondering its options for the 1995 season. When Andy heard the brewery was considering

Riddle's Penultimate. Note sign in window. *Courtesy of Andy Ayers.*

"decking out a crew of sand-lotters and retiree scabs in the hallowed birds-on-bat uniform and calling that abomination 'The St Louis Cardinals' it was too much for me." He promptly dropped all A-B products (garnering considerable press coverage) and didn't resume selling them until after the regular season was underway. Note the sign on the window in the accompanying photograph.

In 2008, the Ayerses turned things over to their daughter K.T., who'd been cooking there and then running the kitchen. Andy moved on to become a wholesaler for all his local sources and a slew of new ones he nurtures. The restaurant closed in 2010.

Their magical garlic potatoes recipe can be found in the recipe section.

ROSSINO'S

Did what's now known as St. Louis–style pizza come to be cut in squares because many early pizza restaurants served it on rectangular aluminum pans?

We'll never know, of course. Still, it's not unreasonable to think that thrifty proprietors urging St. Louisans to try this savory pie in the post–World War II era would find military surplus cafeteria trays a good idea. Pizza, of course, had been served in the United States since early in the twentieth century. But it remained an East Coast dish little known elsewhere until after the war. GIs who'd been in Italy were exposed to it and, their palates awakened, began to think about introducing it to their friends.

Among the first places in the Midwest to make pizza was a half-basement on Sarah just north of West Pine. It had held a series of small restaurants, and Amadeo Fiore bought it in 1945. He called it the Melrose, after the apartment building in which it was located. Around 1947, he began making pizza. It might have been an uphill selling job; his advertisements included how to pronounce "peet-sa." But it proved so popular that he moved to a location on Easton Avenue, what is now Martin Luther King Jr. Drive, the next year.

He sold the restaurant on Sarah to Joseph and Louis Parente. They were the first in a series of well-known restaurateurs to pass through the dark little subterrranean spot on their way to recognition. The brothers went on to open Pagliacci's at Kingshighway and Manchester, and then several restaurants using their family name, including Parente's Italian Village.

In 1954, the Parentes passed it on, as well, to two families who combined their last names to christen the restaurant Rossino's. Roy and Nina Russo teamed up with Frank Gianino. It served the standards of Italian American cooking that people had come to expect: veal parmigiana, chicken cacciatore, pastas (mostly spaghetti, with lasagna and a single mostaccioli option) and thin-crust pizza, as well as a few steaks. Those pizzas were rectangular.

In 1963, Roy and Nina's daughter Nancy and her husband, Tom Zimmerman, bought the restaurant. By that time, it had become a hangout for a varied crowd, including plenty of athletes, "particularly short ones," quipped a wit. The ceilings were notoriously low, made even more hazardous by pipes running hither and yon. But it was true. Football Cardinal players were often spotted there, and so was their coach, Charley Winner, a noted trencherman. Coach Winner was the guy who persuaded the kitchen to put the tomato-ey cacciatore sauce on his steak. Other athletes from teams out of the past, like players from the St. Louis Hawks and the St. Louis Browns, as well as the still-thriving baseball Cardinals, made it a regular stop.

One of Nancy's uncles was Mike Faille, who opened Talayna's Pizza, and another uncle was Charlie Gitto, who has two restaurants and who formerly worked at Rossino's. Nancy's sister Mary Rose had married the son of a nearby saloon's owner, Mike Del Pietro, who worked for a while at Rossino's, too. They went on to create not only a self-named restaurant on Hampton but also four children, Michael Jr., Lea, Angela and Marc, all of whom are or have been in the restaurant business. Other servers who weren't related

Left: Exterior of Rossino's.

Below: Interior of Rossino's. *Courtesy of Toby Weiss/beltstl.com.*

to the family included Kim Tucci, Joe Fresta and John Ferrara, who banded together to open the Pasta Houses, and there are more distant ties to Bob Candicci and the Bardolinos.

Yes. St. Louis really *is* a small town.

The restaurant itself was indeed dark and full of atmosphere. There were red checkered tablecloths and candles—including, if memory serves, some of those fiaschi Chianti bottles with candlewax dripped down the sides from weeks of candles. It felt like a hideaway, a sort of insider place that could have been tucked away below a brownstone on a side street in Manhattan. At any moment, it seemed as though Frank Sinatra and a couple of friends could walk in and be greeted as regulars. As the years passed, the collection of items, both pictures and other things, grew, just the way it would at most homes in the same family for generations.

While Sinatra apparently never made it, another very well-known singer did. In 1988, a guy named Gordon Sumner did. That's right, Sting came to dinner, and the restaurant closed for the night. It seems that Nancy Zimmerman's daughter Natalie had dated Sting's manager for a while.

Nancy decided to shut it down in late 2005. The rush of customers demanding one final meal kept it open another six months or so, but they finally turned off the stoves for the last time in April 2006. Its influence lives on.

RUGGERI'S RESTAURANT

"Nobody goes there any more. It's too crowded."

Was the most famous funny line from longtime New York Yankees catcher Yogi Berra really about Ruggeri's Restaurant? There's no absolute proof of it, but St. Louis, particularly longtime residents with memories of the restaurant and the Italian neighborhood known as The Hill, like to think so.

Ruggeri's was the first of the cluster of Italian restaurants located in the neighborhood. Opened in 1904 by Antonio Ruggeri on the corner of Edwards Avenue at Elizabeth, it appears as though it at first served as a general store as well. Antonio had a son, Henrico, or Henry, who served in World War I and then came home to help his father. Antonio died in 1927, and Henry and his wife, Ermina, took over things.

It was Henry who brought the restaurant to the size and popularity that it reached at its peak. In 1935, he put in an outdoor garden for diners, complete with entertainment. Business was so good that in just two years he took the garden's space for an additional dining area. Ermina, or

Minnie, was a significant part of the success. Many of her recipes became customer favorites, and she oversaw the staff with a warm and maternal hand, including making sure her "boys," the waitstaff, were successfully married off.

Even during the years of World War II and its rationing, they carried on, serving more pasta and fewer of the steaks the restaurant was also known for. The restaurant was such a St. Louis standard by then that the *St. Louis Star and Times* ran a brief note announcing the name of the first Ruggeri's waiter to be drafted, Dan Puricelli. In all, thirteen employees served during the war.

In the summer of 1944, Italian prisoners of war working at the St. Louis Ordnance Depot on North Broadway were allowed, under guard, to go to Mass at St. Ambrose Catholic Church in The Hill neighborhood. After a sermon in Italian by Reverend Fiorenzo Lupo, the pastor, they were taken to Ruggeri's and served breakfast. A large crowd gathered outside the church, but things remained calm.

Henry, as noted, had served in World War I. On the night of August 13, 1945, the restaurant had closed as usual. Shortly after midnight, word got back to the United States that Japan had surrendered. Henry reopened his restaurant for revelers; while the official V-J Day would be August 15, St. Louisans began celebrating immediately in a big way long before daybreak on the fourteenth. Because he was in the service when World War I had ended, Henry explained, he never got to celebrate the way he wanted to. This time, he could.

Ruggeri's was popular in the thirties, but in the economic boom that followed the war, it drew a lot of attention from celebrities—musicians, athletes, broadcasters. It also caught a couple of celebrities on their way up. It often hired from the neighborhood, including from two families named Garagiola and Berra. Henry had noticed by 1942 that one of the Garagiola boys had athletic talents. Joseph was sixteen and already playing for the Springfield (Missouri) Cardinals farm club, a system created by Branch Rickey, and Henry pointed out his prowess in a newspaper interview. Joseph's older brother Mickey worked for Ruggeri's before the war and returned afterward to spend a career there as a waiter. John Berra, who, like the Garagiolas, lived on Elizabeth Avenue, was another who got a job there and ended up as a waiter. Mickey's younger brother Joe, and John's, who was nicknamed Yogi, both became famous catchers and remained well known throughout their lives. But in their early years in professional ball, in the off-season, both of them at one time or another donned a jacket and worked at Ruggeri's. In those days, such jobs were the norm, because baseball salaries weren't enough to make a good living. Mickey took over from Joe to broadcast the popular *Wrestling at the Chase* on Channel 11, and his face became known to non-diners as well.

Another favorite local personality was Stan Kann, who later became known as the funny guy with vacuum cleaners on *The Tonight Show with Johnny Carson*. Kann, an organist at churches and the Fox Theatre, bought an organ at the old Loew's State theater. He had it installed in Ruggeri's basement. He opened just before New Year's Eve 1956 and played there for twenty years, his name becoming almost synonymous with Ruggeri's.

The organ arrived a year after another big expansion at the restaurant, which meant a seating capacity of 650 people, more room for families to celebrate anniversaries, groups to hold meetings and couples to drop by after a show. St. Louis stayed open later in those days.

Henry lived above the restaurant until his death in 1961. Henry Jr. took the helm, but he passed away in 1975. The struggle to stay open began. After being for sale for two years, Ruggeri's finally closed on June 8, 1982.

SCHNAIDER'S BEER GARDEN

It's impossible to talk about St. Louis and not talk about beer. It's so associated with the city that outsiders are often surprised to learn the city's founders were French, not German, and that the territory was a French possession. Our German roots, though, go deep, and while it's harder to find a German restaurant, beer is clearly a big deal around town, both making and consuming it.

Another thing many people don't know is that there were plenty of caves in St. Louis. (They're still there, for the most part, the entrances sealed and concealed.) Beer and caves go together well. The cooler temperatures preferred by the yeast used for lagers made caves a natural brewing asset. Breweries would plant trees around their caves' openings in order to shade them and create even more coolness. Shady? Cool in the summer? Why not put out chairs and maybe some tables for customers to quaff the local product? Voila (it's the same word in German), there's a beer garden.

Perhaps St. Louis's most notable was Schnaider's Beer Garden. Joseph Schnaider had come from Germany and been a partner in the Green Tree Brewery. But in 1865, he sold his interest and bought land at Twentieth and Chouteau to open his own place. And what a place it was. Besides the brewery,

Entrance to Schnaider's Beer Garden. *Courtesy of Missouri Historical Society.*

Really Golden Oldies

Schnaider's Beer Garden, circa 1880s. *Courtesy of Missouri Historical Society.*

there were landscaped gardens, walks, three music pavilions and food—served at the tables, of course. The style must have been similar to European spas, where strolling, listening to music and sipping the liquid being produced, whether mineral water or beer, drew elegant, well-dressed people.

There doesn't seem to be information on what they ate with the beer. Surely there were sausages, whether on rolls or with bread as part of a platter. Visions of trays of pork knuckle *mit* potato dumplings and sauerkraut carried by bustling waiters float through our imagination, but we'll never know.

What we do know is that they had serious entertainment, not just oompah bands. It's been hinted that the roots of the St. Louis Symphony came from one of the bands at Schnaider's. There were light opera performances by their own company, and theater groups performed. It was busy enough that schedules and even reviews were published in the newspapers. Firework displays punctuated the evenings.

Joseph Schnaider died in 1881 on a visit back to Germany, but his wife and son carried on. The brewery and its facilities had acquired a national reputation, although attendance began to falter slightly because of another attraction: baseball. In 1885, the St. Louis team finished first in its league and won the championship series against Chicago. A gigantic parade ensued; contemporary accounts reckon a quarter-million people turned out for it. The parade ended at Schnaider's, where a thousand ticketed guests were served a celebratory meal. By this time, the family had added more buildings, like an icehouse and a summer theater.

But, just like today, consolidation began to occur, and in 1889, the family sold to the St. Louis Brewing Association, joining seventeen other breweries. In 1893, the brewery and the beer garden closed.

Only one building remains today, the malt house. Owned by Paul and Wendy Hamilton, it holds their restaurants, including Vin de Set and PW Pizza, plus a catering facility, Moulin. They honor the building's history. And they've opened a brewpub next door.

STAN MUSIAL AND BIGGIE'S STEAK HOUSE

Another athlete merely sticking his name on a restaurant? That was definitely not the case with Stan Musial and Biggie's. Early in 1949, eight years after Stan Musial was brought up from the minors by the St. Louis Cardinals, he purchased a half interest in Biggie's Restaurant, owned by Julius "Biggie" Garagnani. Located on Chippewa west of Hampton, it specialized in steaks and Italian food.

Renamed Stan Musial and Biggie's Steak House, the opening announcement included the news that Stanley Kann was at the organ. (For more on Kann, see the entry for Ruggieri's.) Musial took his investment seriously. He'd moved his family to St. Louis and frequently mingled with patrons, maintaining an office there. Several times, he told interviewers that his favorite subject in high school had been accounting. He liked keeping the eatery up to date; the decor was redone about every three years. Throughout the restaurant's existence, residents of Donora, Pennsylvania, Musial's hometown, could eat free, provided they had identification.

In its first year, Joe Garagiola, then the catcher for the Cardinals and eventually a television personality, and his bride, Audrie, held their wedding breakfast at the restaurant. By 1952, an ad in the sports section of the *Post-Dispatch* announced that Mickey Garagiola was associated with the restaurant. Joe's brother was a well-known waiter around town and later did some sports announcing locally.

The big change came when the restaurant moved to a new custom-built location at 5130 Oakland Avenue across from Forest Park. The main floor held a cocktail lounge that seated 84 and a dining room with 225 seats. Upstairs were two private rooms, the Colonial seating 300 and the Imperial seating 175. The venue proved to be very popular for all kinds of soirees, from benefits for charities to Democratic Party fundraisers. It was busy at lunch with business types and ran shuttles to Cardinals games until the Redbird Express, the public bus service to games, had a regular stop there, the last stop before heading directly to Busch Stadium. "It was," recalled a regular, thinking of his youth, "a good place to take a date after the theater." People recall the chicken cacciatore.

Lunch menu from Stan Musial and Biggie's, perhaps 1950s. *Courtesy of Special Collections, St. Louis Public Library.*

There was always a chance of running into Stan, of course, who would sometimes whip out his harmonica for a little impromptu round of "Take Me Out to the Ballgame." He retired from playing baseball in 1963. The next year, the team won the World Series. Police had to be called out that evening after the final afternoon game to control the crowd that came to watch the players arrive for the party there. In 1967, Stan became general manager of the team, but the year was clouded by the death of Biggie Garagnani in June. Nevertheless, the team went to the World Series again. The restaurant, noted the *Post-Dispatch*, had installed eight television sets for the occasion, a number remarkable for the time, and the restaurant again hosted the official celebration. Stan stepped down as GM to handle the restaurant and his other business commitments full-time.

One day in May, there was a fire at the restaurant while Stan was at the Kentucky Derby, and employees poured in to straighten the mess up. It opened that same night for dinner.

During the 1982 World Series, Stan came in with Al Hirt, the trumpet player. Dick Balsano was at the piano that night, as he frequently was. Hirt must have had his trumpet at hand, because he sat in. Then Stan pulled out his harmonica, and they played a while. One diner, while leaving, asked who the trio was, and were they there all the time?

For a while, there was a second Musial and Biggie's at the Airport Hilton, one of the hotels that Musial and Biggie's son Jack had an interest in. But

Advertisement, Stan Musial and Biggie's. *Courtesy of Donald M. Casalone.*

the mother ship closed in 1986, the Hilton branch earlier. Musial, a kind, gracious man, stayed in St. Louis and remains a beloved icon today, years after his death.

THE SUNSHINE INN

Arguments break out among fans of the late Sunshine Inn as to what the best dish was. The originally little spot on South Euclid just before Laclede Avenue aroused passions. Not just vegetarian (no one had much heard of the word "vegan" in 1974, when the restaurant opened), it also eschewed coffee, alcohol, desserts and smoking. All of those gradually worked their way into the Sunshine Inn as time passed, though.

In the beginning, there were only twelve tables in the storefront. It faced west, and not surprisingly, given the decor of the seventies, plenty of plants graced the interior and soaked up the afternoon sun. The booths, tables and chairs were wood, and the walls were brick. T-shirts and jeans were the un-uniform of the decade, long hair tied back in ponytails and head wraps when fashion choices or sheer necessity demanded. Except for the aprons, it was often difficult to tell servers from the mostly young clientele. Establishment types sometimes came in, looked around and left. Other times, the departure came after they had read the menu. Eventually, though, the charm of the place and the repeated praising of the food brought in folks beyond the denim brigades. They often remained steady patrons.

In 1978, meat (but not red meat), fish and alcohol appeared on the menu, and cigarettes appeared in the restaurant—with the acknowledgment of the owners, Rudy Nickens and Martha McBroom, that the smoking ban was hurting business. Maybe some patrons left, but more poured in.

What was the best dish? Many would argue that the Golden Lion, a burger made primarily of soybeans and grains, was their favorite, but it's very hard indeed to forget the Garden of Eden salad, featuring greens, of course—never wilted or with the dreaded brown edges—cucumber, red cabbage, carrots, radishes, sprouts, tomato and sunflower seeds. Later, there was a choice of cheese or soy products, as well as dressings, but I remember shreds of white cheddar and a dressing that had lots of parmesan cheese in it. For many, it was a first encounter with both sprouts and sunflower seeds that didn't come in a bag like salted peanuts. The texture was as remarkable as the taste.

Other dishes float through the memory. Cream cheese on date bread with fresh fruit. Iced red zinger tea. Chocolate mousse, probably its first appearance at a popularly priced restaurant in town (with apologies to Balaban's, several blocks north). These weren't low-fat foods, but they were delicious. *The Moosewood Cookbook* came out the year the Sunshine Inn opened. Here was, in effect, our own place to explore that world.

It expanded next door in 1984. Did that seem to change things? Another question for vigorous discussion. There was a certain loss of camaraderie, it seemed. Things finally came to a halt in 1998 in a rent dispute, and we all left the Garden of Eden at 8½ South Euclid for the last time.

The recipe for the Garden of Eden salad dressing is in the recipe section.

THE THREE FOUNTAINS

Like many happening neighborhoods, it's difficult to pinpoint exactly when Gaslight Square began to exist as a spot for bars, restaurants and music in addition to the antiques stores already there. But there's general agreement that the tornado in February 1959 was the yeast that made things seriously expand. There was a lot of damage. But there was insurance money, and it gave capital so that buildings could be repaired and updated.

One place that did the Cinderella thing was the old Musical Arts Building, owned at the time of the tornado by a family named Mutrux. A young Helen Traubel, who sang at the Metropolitan Opera and went on to do television and cabaret, took voice lessons there. Vincent Price, best known for his roles in horror films, as a boy went to a dentist in the building. (No remarks about black capes flapping, please.) In 1953, Richard Mutrux opened the Gaslight Bar in the building. The establishment eventually lent its name to the intersection of Olive Street at Boyle and the surrounding area.

The 1959 tornado took the roof off of the Musical Arts Building, just as one had done thirty-two years earlier. This time, though, the rehab was quite a bit different. Richard and his brother Paul Mutrux sank $250,000 into it (more than $2 million today).

Today, we'd say they recycled. In those days, it was just being quirky, and having a good eye for lovely old things. Urban redevelopment had taken the once-fashionable area called the Mill Creek Valley, which had become a slum. Just east of Grand and south of Olive, the homes had been razed. Eventually, the area would become LaClede Town, LaClede Park and Operation Breakthrough, but that's another story—and they, too, are now gone. The wrecking companies that operated as the houses were taken apart had salvaged quite a bit, and the Mutrux brothers began shopping.

Cypress paneling and doors with beveled glass lined the walls of the two-story restaurant they would call the Three Fountains. Reclaimed stained glass was backlit, and a plethora of chandeliers whose life had begun in the British Building at the Louisiana Purchase Exposition of 1904 shed light on things. The backbar was a mantel from a home at the southwest corner of Lindell and Taylor Avenues that had been demolished; other pieces from the same house were also utilized.

It was elegant, and it was unlike anything St. Louis had seen up until then.

This was still the Midwest, though, so the menu had plenty of beef on it as well as a couple of chicken entrées, pork being considered a tad too workaday for fancy

Advertisement, Three Fountains. *Courtesy of Donald M. Casalone.*

menus. And, to be safe, there were five different preparations of potatoes on the menu. But there was also duckling with the diner's choice of orange or cherry sauce. Frog legs, an old St. Louis favorite, showed up, and so did sweetbreads. Speaking of what's now called "variety meats," Paul's recipe for tripes a la mode de Caen was in the *Post-Dispatch* food section, the tripe being slowly simmered with a cow's hoof to make the stock even richer.

While the restaurant drew national celebrities as well as piles of locals, not everyone was crazy about it. Craig Claiborne, the restaurant critic from the *New York Times*, visited St. Louis and seemed mostly to visit the steak houses, then at the peak of their popularity. But a trip to the Three Fountains left him with, so to speak, a bad taste in his mouth. "It is said to be the only French restaurant in the city, and if it is true, it is unfortunate."

St. Louis has tended not to worry about what New York thinks, and that was the case here. Besides, the Mutrux family had raised the boys and their ten siblings in Europe for a few years before returning to St. Louis, and both Richard and Paul, plus Paul's twin, George, had lived in France after World War II. George, in fact, had a restaurant in Paris.

The party went on from just before Christmas in 1960 until 1968, as urban unrest took its toll on business. There was talk of it moving downtown, but there seems to be no trace of that ever coming to fruition. Richard stayed in St. Louis. Paul, who was an architect, went to Acapulco for a while and opened a restaurant called Los Tres Fontanas. He ended up in San Francisco, where his daughter Michelle became a chef and for a while had a restaurant, the Wappo Bar, in Calistoga, in Napa County's wine country. She made sure it had a fountain—in honor, she said, of the family's tradition.

TONY FAUST'S OYSTER HOUSE & RESTAURANT

The granddaddy of great St. Louis restaurants was, without a doubt, Tony Faust's Oyster House & Restaurant. Anthony R. Faust opened it in 1868 (or 1871; accounts vary). He was a German émigré who'd been a plasterer but was shot in the leg by accident in 1861. Shortly thereafter, he opened a restaurant at Broadway and Russell. The move to Broadway and Elm was the start of the big time for him. It was next to the luxurious Southern Hotel and across from the Olympic Theatre.

It soon gained a national reputation for fine dining and lovely surroundings. In 1877, though, a terrible fire at the Southern Hotel cost thirty-one people their lives and did much damage to Faust's establishment. When he reopened, it was even more elegant than before. Long before the current revival of outdoor dining in restaurants, Faust set up a rooftop garden, under a canopy in the daytime. (St. Louis sun! Heavy Victorian clothing!) At night, it was open to the stars. He also added a market selling delicacies like the oysters for which he was known.

But even that wasn't enough for Faust. In 1887, he rebuilt the restaurant from the basement up, drawing on his tours through Europe. The separate dining room for women, which had been in existence in the previous restaurant, was placed on the second floor with its own entrance.

Who was eating there, and what was on the table? The most important guest from our standpoint was Adolphus Busch, the brewer, who lunched there every day. And he drank wine, not beer, noted contemporary accounts. Busch and Faust became close friends. Not only did the brewery create and widely sell a beer named Faust, but also Busch's daughter married Edward Faust, one of Tony's sons. Business leaders—who were also leaders of society—flocked there for lunches and dinners. Theater people, including the leading actors of the time like Joseph Jefferson, Maude Adams and the first generation of the Barrymore family of thespians supped after performances across the street. In 1901, Emma Goldman, described by the *St. Louis Republic* as "the woman anarchist," was said to have held a conference with St. Louis sympathizers at Tony Faust's. The revolution, had it happened, would have been well fed.

It's important to note that by the time Faust's opened, mechanical ice-making machines had been around for a couple of decades. That's why he was able to bring in not just oysters but other seafood as well, like Spanish mackerel, appreciated as a delicacy and as expensive as lobster on his bill of fare. He also established a cannery on his property to can oysters, something that had been done since before 1850.

But the food went well beyond seafood. Frog legs, woodcock and other game, chanterelle mushrooms and *spaghetti à l'italienne* were offered at one time or another. Eventually, the menu even evolved to having separate sections for fresh vegetables and canned. Surprisingly, curry powder was in use from time to time. It was the sort of thing that the market offered for sale. Joseph Jefferson ordered quail with sauerkraut one night, startling the kitchen, but it soon became a specialty of the house, and quail-eating contests were held from time to time. Faust was once fined for selling game out of season, which gave him no pause at all.

Faust died in 1906 on an extended visit to Germany. He had traveled often and left the restaurant in the hands of capable employees and another son, also named Anthony. But Anthony's health was also poor. In 1911, his wife had him declared incompetent, and he died the following year. St. Louis's entertainment district was moving west, and on the last day of June 1916, the restaurant closed. The building remained until 1933, when it was razed. Even then, the event brought enough notice that the *Saint Louis Star and Times* published in its letters column a poem from a reader saying goodbye to it.

But bits of it lingered on for a long time. For a while, a saloon in the suburb of Overland was said to have had the twenty-four-foot backbar from the restaurant, and it ended up in a garage. That may have been the same piece that Tom Burnham put into his Key West Cafe when Union Station reopened in 1985. Beer and oysters…the bar must have felt right at home.

WILD'S PALACE OF POISON

A brave man, Art Wild, named his restaurant Wild's Palace of Poison when he opened it in 1947. He was also known for having a good sense of humor, and that surely must have been true. A skull-and-crossbones neon sign topped the white building, and another sign proclaimed "Eat Here If It Kills You."

Aside from the jokes, it was a pretty classic drive-in, complete with young women carhops—there was no inside seating—and a short menu. But the joke, particularly pungent when one considered its location, directly across Lemay Ferry Road from Mount Hope Cemetery, played well with teenagers just beginning to come into their own in the years after World War II. The tension and worry—and the gasoline and meat rationing—were past. It was definitely time for a laugh.

Wild went so far as to explain his phone number as HUdson "nine ate, nine sick" (9896) in those days of four-digit numbers. The menu had murder burgers and suicide burgers, the latter without onion. Chili went by "phantom's kiss," a "scorpion's sting" was a hot dog with barbecue sauce, and the "ptomaine special" was a ham and cheese. Soda was called "arsenic fizz." Interestingly, French fries had no special title.

It was hardly a place of licentious living, other than perhaps Junior squealing tires in Dad's Oldsmobile as the young squire headed out to take his date home. The restaurant had milk-drinking contests, for crying out loud.

The crowning touch, or perhaps we should say the fatal touch, was a souvenir available for the asking. It was a faux death certificate, filled with more morbid silliness.

Things went well until a Steak 'n Shake was built in the next block. Wild's Palace of Poison finally bit the dust for real in 1964.

ZINNIA

Purple. For years, my husband and I, working for the Zagat guides, read the comments made by diners rating St. Louis restaurants. Every edition, there would be multiple people using that word about Zinnia in the extremely limited space available for comments. It certainly was purple, although a pastel shade. The next most-common comment was, "former gas station." That was true, too. But neither of those were the most important thing about Zinnia.

It was all about the food. Oh, the service was nice, and the interior walls were more subdued than the amethyst exterior. The artwork was pleasantly rowdy, like the Theresa Disney portrait of owners David Guempel and Larry Adams' Welsh corgis. But the food, and the handy location en route to Webster University's Loretto-Hilton Center for theater and opera, were a winning combination. On opening nights in particular, reservations were in high demand, and there was always a fair amount of table-hopping on those evenings.

David ran the kitchen. He had been at Balaban's, and Duff's before that, a fine curriculum vitae for a place like this. Larry handled the front of the house, and a word on entering made sure that a table could skedaddle in time for a curtain with no difficulty at all. Plenty of specials, but more importantly to the locals, certain dishes that were guaranteed to be on the menu, caused a delicious agony. The cold mussels in a dill sauce were always popular, and wee duck tacos in wonton shells with a mango salsa practically marched right into a diner's waiting mouth. The kitchen had a dab hand with seafood, whether it was a variety of fish and shellfish in a paella-esque rendition or softshell crabs lightly sauteed in butter with some bread to mop up the juices. The kitchen was also gracious enough to remove the bone from each lamb shank before it was served, a fine and rare idea. Zinnia was also perhaps the only restaurant in town to routinely offer sweetbreads (not pastry; the thymus and pancreas glands, usually of a calf) on its menu. Preparation varied, but it was popular enough to be a standard item on their *carte*.

An excellent sticky toffee pudding with a crème anglaise sauce became a regular offering, too. But sometimes passing dishes stay in the memory, like a strawberry shortcake made with tender slices of angel food cake that had been toasted on the grill, caramelizing a little of the sugar in the cake. Unforgettable.

Eventually, a section of the building, previously a small dining room, was turned into a bar, and Guempel and Adams brought in Karen Devine, a popular bartender from another restaurant, Redel's. Devine remembers the bar seeming to create a club-like atmosphere, inviting conversation and friendships. Behind the building, a narrow porch was created or enlarged, extremely private but very cool from the closely surrounding vegetation, feeling more like a holiday home than a night in Webster Groves.

Zinnia was open for eighteen years, with lots of devoted fans. It closed in March 2008.

Part III
Still Open for Business

Here's a trio of really old restaurants that are still around and very interesting. Two of them are still in the founding families. All three are worthwhile for various reasons.

AL'S RESTAURANT

First and Biddle Streets, St. Louis, MO 63102
314-421-6399
www.alsrestaurant.net

Al's Restaurant is an unremarkable-looking building, dwarfed by the ancient Union Light and Power Company building, whose dusty Beaux-Arts presence still impresses, the way it must have for the 1904 World's Fair. The power station still works, too, producing the steam that circulates through downtown St. Louis, sometimes weaving its way up manhole covers.

Al's is, in some ways, the same—old but still working—although definitely minus any dust or grime. Aside from reupholstering the comfortable chairs in the dining room, it's not changed a great deal in several decades. The building was originally a sugar warehouse that had become a saloon. Al Baroni delivered soda water to it regularly, and in 1925, owner Julius Vogel offered to sell it to Baroni. Louise Baroni, Al's wife, thought this was an excellent idea, and the couple purchased it. Al kept driving the soda truck, at least for a while, and Louise began to run the business, including offering simple lunches. At the time they opened, she was pregnant with their son, who would be Albert Jr. Louise must have been quite a powerhouse.

They lived above the restaurant. Business was good. Steamboats docked up and down the riverfront a block away, and there was a steel mill nearby. Lunch in particular was a busy time, with lines of people waiting to be fed. Eventually, in the evenings, the steam table was turned off, tablecloths put out and waiters in long aprons said, "Here's what we've got tonight," reeling off five or six main courses. It was still pretty casual, but they were selling steaks even back in the thirties.

Louise was in charge for forty years, until her death in 1965. At that time, Al Jr. took over.

The restaurant had survived Prohibition, the Depression and World War II with its rationing of meat and gasoline. It was a fixture on the riverfront. But there was more to come, and this time, it would be close to home—very close to home, indeed. On the morning of January 10, 1968, a fast-moving fire destroyed a bag company just north of Al's. The building completely collapsed, taking the north wall of Al's with it. At the time of the fire, the temperature was twelve degrees.

Who knows if Al Jr. had a bright idea in the aftermath of the fire or if he'd been thinking about this for a while? He reopened in six months. He'd removed the top story from the building and completely remodeled it. Lunch was dropped, and things went from homey to quite upscale.

The "new" Al's thrived. It was not just a special-occasion restaurant but was popular with businessmen entertaining important clients and visiting celebrities. In this sports-crazy town, it frequently fed professional athletes, umpires and referees. During the years that the football Cardinals were based here, it was a regular Saturday night stop for visiting sports journalists. Big-name stars from the Muny dropped by. Henry Fonda was a regular, and Al Jr. would drive him home. But the only celebrity photo in the dining room is that of Frank Sinatra with his dog. Sinatra apparently ate there whenever he was in town, and once, eating alone, he ordered two steaks. No, he told Al, he wasn't expecting anyone. Al, after numerous previous visits from "Ol' Blue Eyes," felt comfortable quizzing him on the second steak. His dog, it turns out, was with Sinatra's driver in the waiting car. Al, notorious in his family for his affection for dogs, insisted that the dog be brought in as well, and all ended happily. Sinatra's picture hangs over the corner table where the dog and his owner had their steaks.

The bar at Al's Restaurant feels like a riverboat. *Author's photo.*

Al Jr., too, gave the restaurant forty years. After his death in 2005, his daughter Pam Baroni Neal and her husband, Gary Neal, took over. They've kept most of the traditions and the longtime employees. Another scare occurred in 2015. The city wanted to put a new stadium just north of downtown, near the river. Al's would have been replaced by a parking lot. But agreement could not be reached over funding, among other things, and Stan Kroenke's Rams took their balls back to California.

The dark-paneled dining room is set off by white tablecloths and black-tie servers. Private wine lockers bear some well-known names. The bar, a post-fire creation, is striking. The feel is of sitting on a covered deck of a steamboat, looking at the riverfront of St. Louis in the late 1800s, thanks to a mural from Nate Ettlinger, who was a scenic designer at what is now the Muny.

The tradition of a spoken menu certainly continues. Al tried a written menu for a little while, but longtime customers didn't care for it. Main courses have a visual aid, a large tray of steaks, chops and seafood for inspection. It can be confusing for newcomers and those who don't visit often, but the servers are patient. In addition, the general rule is, "If you want something not on the menu, we'll make it for you, as long as we have the ingredients on hand," once an accepted wisdom at many restaurants in this price range around town. The website has a menu of the usual options, but sometimes things like softshell crab come and go.

And that brings us to another point. The prices are not mentioned at all unless requested. It's not quite the old line, "If you have to ask, you can't afford it," but this isn't a mid-price restaurant. In recent months, dinner for two with first courses has been talked about between $200 and $350. But, of course, one never knows how much people drank, something that can drastically affect a bill.

But whatever you do, whatever you eat, get the onion rings, the single must-have dish. That, and maybe a glass of sparkling wine while you ease into the rhythm of an important evening, should work out very well.

BEVO MILL

4749 Gravois, St. Louis, MO 63116
314-832-2251
www.dasbevo.com

Bevo Mill: A mill, yes, or at least built to look like a mill, with its long arms turning lazily. But *Bevo*? What, or who, was Bevo? Bevo was a made-up word, the name of a product of Anheuser-Busch. The word seems to have come from combining "beverage" and *pivo*, the Slavic word for beer. The brewery began producing the nearly non-alcoholic drink in 1916, when alcoholic beverages were prohibited by the American armed forces. It was the best-known of the near-beers that came on the market to try to keep breweries afloat, so to speak, during Prohibition, which began in 1920. At that point, of course, they removed the scant remaining alcohol content.

St. Louisans may be familiar with the Anheuser-Busch building at Broadway and Arsenal. On each corner, a fox perches casually, holding a chicken drumstick and a mug. That fox with crossed ankles was sometimes called Bevo, although he was based on Reynard, the trickster of the fables. Yes, before Louie the Lizard and even the Clydesdales, there was a fox in the A-B ads. You'll see him, of course, at Bevo Mill.

Until the Gateway Arch was erected, Bevo Mill was as much the emblem of St. Louis as the statue of Louis IX in front of the St. Louis Art Museum.

Bevo Mill around the time of its opening. *Courtesy of Missouri Historical Society.*

The immense faux windmill remains a landmark more than one hundred years after its construction. On the site of a blacksmith's shop, it was built for August A. Busch. For the first couple of years after its construction, it served as a private club for his entertaining. The Mill is roughly halfway between the brewery and the Busch family home at Grant's Farm, although it's hard to credit the stories that it was a place to spend the night en route. Mr. Busch was fond of Pierce-Arrow automobiles, big and luxurious, and it's not like he had to drive himself.

It was opened to the public with much fanfare in June 1917. Mr. Busch opined that the solution to "the saloon problem" was the German family garden, where only beer and light wine are served with meals. The *St. Louis Post-Dispatch* story about the opening dryly pointed out that the restaurant felt like a country club but the views out the windows showed washing hung up to dry and tin baby bathtubs on balconies. Moreover, continued the nameless ink-stained wretch, servers so strongly encouraged the consumption of Bevo, beer or wine, that diners were charged five cents for water.

Cynicism aside, it was a handsome building, and immediately popular. It can still be visited. On the main floor, to the right of the foyer opens a large beamed hall with a fireplace, the sort of place where the Valkyries might have a long, festive meal. There's an unsubstantiated story that Mr. Busch built the fireplace himself with rock he brought in by the carload from Grant's Farm. At the base of each beam, look for the carved heads in the style of medieval decorative architecture. Each head is different, each doing something with food or drink, except one fellow who has a postprandial pipe.

To the left of the foyer is the round room that's directly under the blades of the windmill. Originally Mr. Busch's private dining room, it's much lighter than the larger room, but the most impressive features are hidden until the visitor walks in and turns around. Two murals on porcelain came from the old Tony Faust's restaurant. They'd been made in Berlin and were shown at the World's Columbian Exhibition in Chicago in 1893. Faust bought them and shipped them here. After the restaurant closed, Busch acquired them. For a while in the 1950s, they were covered up with paneling.

Downstairs was the bar, known for a while as the Yacht Club, with live music. Charley Hartig's Alpine Band put in appearances in 1939. It became the Bavarian Room in 1961.

That same year, the Schneithorst family took over the restaurant. They put up new blades for the windmill, the old ones having been removed for safety reasons years before. When Arthur Schneithorst, the patriarch, died

Left: Decorative carving at Bevo Mill. The figure has a mug of Bevo in his hand. *Author's photo*.

Below: Window in Bevo Mill's main dining room. Note the Bevo characters. *Author's photo*.

in 1947, his wife, Bertha, took the reins and lived in an apartment on the second floor directly under the windmill. She's quoted as saying she never tasted the food, because she knew it was always good.

What came out of the kitchen over the years? The menu that first year with the Schneithorsts in charge seemed to be rather eclectic; among one week's daily specials were chop suey and hassenpfeffer. The ad didn't need to explain either dish, although nowadays the German rabbit stew is hardly a household word. Steaks, chicken and seafood were mainstays.

German dishes were apparently always there, too. However, it's clear that how many were on the menu at any given time varied over the years. They waxed and waned depending on their popularity and the restaurateurs' guess about that popularity. Spaetzle dumplings, for instance, were dropped because they were being ignored in favor of potato pancakes. Crawfish soup was a mainstay on the menu, and so was rotisserie chicken. "Sooper Dooper Lobster" was touted frequently in ads, even before the 1953 addition of a tank to show off the live crustaceans. Soon, a freshwater tank was added to allow patrons to catch their own trout, foregoing a fly rod for a net. Apple strudel and house-made rolls came from a longtime employee who did nothing but bake.

The Schneithorst lease on the restaurant ended in 1959, and they passed the lease to Collins Enterprises, a group that provided food in industrial settings. That began a series of closings and changes. In 1980, sportscaster Jack Buck attempted to get the lease, long before he and his family began J Buck's. Kym and Associates took over the restaurant, with considerable change to the menu, in 1982. It closed in 1984. In 1986, experienced restaurateurs Patrick Hanon and Ray Gallardo remodeled and reopened it, but struggled. By 2001, it was open only on weekends and mostly acted as a venue for private functions. Anheuser-Busch, by then no longer belonging to the Busch family, gave the land to the City of St. Louis in 2009, and the restaurant closed, seemingly for good, three months later.

Restaurateurs are an optimistic group. In 2017, Pat and Carol Schuchard bought the building and the land from the city and have reopened it as Das Bevo. The beer garden area on the north side of the building shows a sense of humor, much like City Museum, although on a much smaller scale. And they clearly love the interior. The upstairs apartments are going to be used for private functions, and there's murmuring about a bed-and-breakfast.

The building, under whatever name, will always be an essential part of St. Louis nostalgia.

Still Open for Business

CROWN CANDY KITCHEN

1401 St. Louis Avenue, St. Louis, MO 63106
314-621-9650
www.crowncandykitchen.net

Self-indulgence by its very nature is a highly personal thing. Some people think the height of doing what they want is skydiving, or spending hours at a slot machine. It could be a new boat or going to a spa. But when it comes to self-indulgence at the table, there's near-universal agreement in St. Louis about the importance of one of our oldest spots.

Crown Candy Kitchen harkens back to 1913, when Harry Karandzieff, who'd come to this country from Macedonia, bought a building on St. Louis Avenue. Built in 1880, it was first a feed store, then a tailor's shop and a shoe store. Harry decided to make candy his business, not just selling it retail but making it himself. His cousin Pete Jugaloff was working as a carpenter in South St. Louis, and Harry brought him on board. Uncle Pete, as he came to be known to everyone, not only crafted the booths that are still there, but he also helped design the candy cases and the fountain. He also was the fixer for the ice-cream machinery.

The building also served as the family home. Harry married Eleni, also an immigrant from Macedonia, and they had two children, George and Athena, who was known as Tina. Sadly, Eleni died when the children were very small. Harry remarried, in time, to Aristicia, a widow from Chicago, and they had another son, William.

From the start, they included ice cream as well as candy. Vanilla, chocolate and strawberry were the only ice-cream flavors for years. In the early years, all of it was hand-cranked. As to the candy, St. Louis had a number of German émigrés who were willing to pass on their skills, so Harry and Pete watched and learned. They began to acquire the molds that make the chocolate models still filling their case, especially at Easter and Christmas.

Things went well, in no small part due to the hard work of the family. George and Tina began pitching in when they were small. William, who was disabled, also lent a hand when possible. They added plate lunches and then dinners. Eventually, Tina came to be the one who ran the kitchen. She was the one who believed in sandwiches, the lighter lunch that could be—pardon the phrase—crowned with an ice-cream treat. George absorbed the candy- and ice-cream-making techniques and philosophy, and he charmed customers.

The fountain at Crown Candy Kitchen. *Author's photo.*

George, back from World War II, where he drove a tank for General Patton, married Bessie De Polito. He began to assume more responsibilities, and Tina eventually left the kitchen to raise her own family. Harry and Uncle Pete didn't retire, but the fresh young blood gave them a chance to catch their breath. And even more young blood began to arrive, George's sons Tommy, Mike and Andy.

As the boys got older, George was finally able to relax a little and would travel the Midwest looking for more Coca-Cola memorabilia to add to what the store had accumulated over the years. He never went without bringing along chocolate, says the family, to sweeten the deal. George passed away in 2005. His death was marked by an editorial in the *St. Louis Post-Dispatch* saluting him.

Even before the loss of George, the sons were stepping up to the plate. Mike, the firstborn, eventually took over making almost all the ice cream and began acting as the soda jerk. Mom Bessie said Mike was just like his dad, driven and a perfectionist. He passed away in 2012. Tommy became the successor to Tina, running the kitchen and developing things like the chili recipe. Andy, the youngest, now the most public face of Crown Candy

Kitchen, is there pretty much constantly. His wife, Sherri, handles media inquiries, among many other things. Many of the servers have been working there almost as long as the family members.

The signature dish is the bacon, lettuce and tomato sandwich, a dish that's brought in television crews from across the country. It's all about the bacon, really. They use twelve to fourteen strips, deep-fried in batches, in each one. It wasn't always quite this big; now it's a behemoth that equals the size of a New York delicatessen sandwich. The egg salad and the chili are very popular, but the BLT is the star.

Speaking of stars, the featured ones at Crown Candy are the police. Maybe in other places cops do doughnuts, but in St. Louis, they do ice cream. On 90 percent of my visits, there have been police lunching, leaving and schmoozing—and not just uniformed guys. The next most-notable are the big names. Over the years, the place has hosted everyone from Tony Curtis and Carol Channing to Jimmy Kimmel (his wife's a St. Louisan) and Bill Murray. Murray had a malt and left. But within a couple of hours, he'd phoned in an order for fifty more for his crew. Football Cardinals owner Billy Bidwill brought in NFL commissioner Pete Rozelle. It's a frequent lunch spot for local media folks and political types.

On Christmas Day 1983 in St. Louis it was thirteen degrees below zero. A space heater running to keep pipes from freezing at the store started a fire. Most of the damage was from smoke and heat, but the establishment lost many of the Coca-Cola items and plenty of melted candy. It managed to reopen by the end of January. Uncle Pete's booths, with a new coat of paint much like the old one, survived. The whole store still feels like decades past.

Easter is the busiest time of the year, starting in January, when the rabbit-making kicks into high gear. Rabbits in various poses and sizes, including with an ancient style of motorcycle, and other animals like the Easter monkey, abound. In 2011, the year of baseball's Rally Squirrel, they had a squirrel mold ready in the bullpen when rodent-mania hit. Those traditional, elaborate, heart-shaped boxes for Valentine's Day? They're here, as well as chocolate Santas galore in December. Andy has begun offering misfit chocolate animals, piecing together broken ones, a story that was featured on *NBC Nightly News*.

George Karandzieff always suggested a little nutmeg on the top of a malt, maybe one with the fresh bananas on the counter. To go with the BLT, of course. Go indulge.

Part IV
In Those Kitchens

Elsah Landing: Pumpkin Praline Pie

You're on your own for the pie shell here, although I also think that this might work in a graham cracker crust in a buttered pie pan with maybe a 5-minute pre-bake. Be sure you're using pumpkin, not the canned pumpkin pie mix. "Plain gelatin" means not gelatin dessert, but the unflavored kind, such as Knox makes. This is the original recipe; the amount of pumpkin in a can has been reduced to 15 ounces now, but that'll work just as well. Things will proceed more rapidly if both the eggs and the milk are at room temperature.

The extravagant among us might put a little brandy or bourbon in either the pumpkin mixture or the whipped cream.

1 (9-inch) pie shell, unbaked

Preheat oven to 450 degrees. Bake crust 10 minutes in preheated oven.

⅓ cup butter
⅓ cup brown sugar
⅓ cup pecans, chopped

Cream butter and brown sugar together. Stir in pecans. Spread evenly over bottom of partially baked shell. Bake 5 minutes longer. Cool.

¾ cup sugar
1 envelope plain gelatin
1 teaspoon cinnamon
½ teaspoon ginger
¼ teaspoon cloves
½ teaspoon salt

Combine sugar, gelatin, cinnamon, ginger, cloves and salt in the top of a double boiler.

4 eggs, separated
1 (16-ounce) can pumpkin
¾ cup milk

Beat egg yolks slightly; add with pumpkin and milk to sugar mixture. Mix well. Cook over hot, not boiling water for 15 minutes or until gelatin dissolves. Chill. (Place over a bowl of ice to hasten chilling.) Stir occasionally and continue chilling until mixture starts to thicken and becomes syrupy.

¼ cup sugar

Beat egg whites until fluffy. Gradually beat in sugar until egg whites are thick and glossy. Fold into chilled pumpkin mixture.
Turn filling into the cooled shell.

½ cup whipping cream
1 tablespoon confectioner's sugar

Whip cream until almost stiff. Add confectioner's sugar and continue beating until stiff.

Top pie with whipped cream and chill until serving time.

Makes 1 pie, serves 6–8.

Fio's La Fourchette: Lisa's Chocolate Cake

This recipe is written a little differently than most modern recipes. You'll need to preheat the oven to 375 degrees. The pan called for, a 12-inch round pan, needs to be a pan with removable sides, like those used for cheesecakes.

Fio Antognini told me they use Quaker's Old Fashioned Oats in the cake. The powdered sugar is measured by weight. If you don't have a scale in your kitchen, measuring the powdered sugar is a little tricky. A box of powdered sugar is 16 ounces, and the sugar company C&H considers it as measuring out as 3¾ cups. You want 1/8 of that box, so 0.43 of a cup, or a very scant half cup.

"One of our favorite old Swiss recipes!" said the note from Fio.

Part one:
1 cup warm water
½ cup melted unsalted butter
2 ounces semi-sweet Swiss chocolate (top quality)

Part two:
2 cups oatmeal flakes (not instant) coarsely processed in food processor
1 ½ cups sugar
½ cup all-purpose flour
½ teaspoon baking soda
Pinch of salt
2 eggs
½ cup sour cream

Part three:
4 ounces sweet Swiss chocolate (top quality)
¼ cup heavy cream
2 tablespoons hot water
2 ounces of powdered sugar

In a double boiler, melt part one: water, butter and chocolate. Stir until well blended.

Remove this mixture from double boiler and place in bowl of mixer with all of the part two ingredients. Mix in mixer medium speed until well blended. Pour this mixture into a greased 12-inch round pan lined with parchment paper. Place in preheated 375-degree oven for 35 to 40 minutes.

In double boiler, melt part three chocolate. Once melted, add the powdered sugar, water and cream. Stir until smooth. When the cake is removed from the oven, spread this mixture on top of the cake. Let cool, remove from the pan and serve at room temperature with whipped cream.

Serves 8–12.

The Green Parrot Inn: Fried Chicken

For Green Parrot fried chicken, you should have a chicken that weighs about two pounds after it is dressed and cut up. You will also need a heavy, cast aluminum skillet; not an iron skillet, but a cast aluminum skillet.

Fill the skillet about one-third full of pure lard and let it heat just to a sizzle. Have your chicken cut up and ice cold. Dredge each piece well with salt and pepper, roll in flour and place in the skillet. Do not crowd the pieces. Cover the skillet tightly, turn the fire as high as you can and cook for ten minutes. At the end of ten minutes, look at the chicken; if each piece looks brown around the edge, turn quickly and recover the skillet, and cook to a golden brown.

Do not take each piece out of the skillet when it is browned, but pick up the skillet and drain the grease off before you take up the chicken. This will keep your chicken from being greasy.

Chicken may be kept hot in a very slow oven while gravy is made from the chicken fryings, but it should not be covered tightly enough to cause it to steam, as this will make the crust soft and spongy. Green Parrot fried chicken is always a golden brown, and tender, yet crisp.

Do not substitute vegetable shortening for the pure lard, and be sure your skillet is at least one-third full of lard before you start to cook your chicken.

King Louie's: Chilled Spiced Tomato-Pepper Soup

This is the recipe of Kirk Warner, still around town as a private chef. He suggests serving it with a dollop of crème fraiche and a sprinkle of garlic chives, alongside crostini or garlic toasts. And, he adds, it can also be served hot.

You can find Thai chili sauce at Global Market on Kirkwood Road and other places around St. Louis; substituting a dab of sour cream or even thick Greek yogurt for the crème fraiche wouldn't be heresy.

> 1 shallot, minced
> 1 ¼ teaspoons minced fresh garlic
> 2–3 tablespoons olive oil
> 1 (28-ounce) can Italian plum tomatoes
> 1-2 teaspoons chili sauce (Thai chili sauce preferred)
> 2 teaspoons granulated sugar
> 1 ½–2 cups vegetable stock or chicken stock
> Kosher salt
> Freshly ground multicolored peppercorns

Saute shallot and garlic in olive oil over low heat until transparent. Add tomatoes and chili sauce to taste, sugar, stock, salt and pepper to taste. Cover and simmer about 15 minutes. Chill.

When cold, puree in blender or food processor, working in batches if necessary, leaving small chunks of tomato.

Makes about 6 cups of soup.

Nantucket Cove: Mayfair Dressing

> ½ large onion, peeled and diced
> 1 rib celery, diced
> 1 clove garlic, peeled and crushed
> 2 (2-ounce) cans flat anchovy fillets
> 3 eggs
> 2 tablespoons prepared mustard
> ¼ cup water
> 2 cups safflower oil
> 1 teaspoon cracked black pepper
> 1 teaspoon monosodium glutamate (Accent), optional

Combine all ingredients in a blender. Pulse on low speed until all ingredients are homogenized. Increase speed to high; blend on high speed for 1 minute. (Or use a food processor, pulsing until homogenized and then processing until well combined.)

Parkmoor: Chickburger

The barbecue spice referred to in the recipe is made by Farmer Brothers, a restaurant supply chain. If you use a favorite rub instead, pay attention to the amount of salt and sugar you add, as some rubs are heavy on those.

> 1 pound finely chopped chicken or turkey meat (white or dark)
> 2 tablespoons barbecue spice or to taste
> 5 tablespoons granulated sugar
> 1 tablespoon celery salt
> ¾ teaspoon black pepper
> 10–12 ounces chicken broth

Preheat oven to 350 degrees.

Toss chicken, spices, salt and pepper together in a 9-by-13-inch pan. Cover mixture with the chicken broth. Bake, uncovered, for 35 to 40 minutes or until mixture has a crust on top. It should be moist when removed from the oven. Add a little more broth if needed.

Serve on toasted buns with lettuce, tomato and tartar sauce.

Serves 5–6.

Riddle's Penultimate: Magical Garlic Potatoes

> 2½ pounds red potatoes
> 1½ cups half-and-half
> 3 cups heavy (40 percent) cream
> 1½ ounces (about 2 tablespoons plus 2 teaspoons) minced garlic
> ½ teaspoon salt
> ½ teaspoon white pepper

Preheat oven to 400 degrees. Butter a 9-by-13-inch casserole.

Wash and peel potatoes. Slice ¼ inch thick.

Combine potatoes, half-and-half, cream, garlic, salt and pepper in a saucepan. Bring to a boil over high heat. Reduce heat to a simmer and cook for 6 to 8 minutes.

Pour potatoes and sauce in casserole. Bake until potatoes are soft, about 45 minutes.

Serves 12–15.

The Sunshine Inn: Cheesy Italian Dressing

1 ½ cups safflower oil
½ cup lemon juice
⅓ cup apple cider vinegar
1 small yellow onion, finely chopped
1 medium red tomato, cubed
3 tablespoons tomato juice
1 tablespoon honey
1 ½ cups grated Parmesan cheese

Combine all ingredients in blender. Blend until well mixed. Refrigerate leftovers; remix if necessary before serving.

SAVING THE WORLD, ONE CAT AT A TIME

What I Know About Cats –
And Why You Should Know It, Too

By Rachel S. Geller, Ed.D.
Certified Humane Education Specialist &
Cat Behavior Counselor

As told to
Nancy Shohet West

Copyright © 2019 Nancy Shohet West
www.NancyShohetWest.com
Cover design by Kristine Zards Rencs
All rights reserved.
ISBN: 9781090130273

Foreword: Married to the Cat Lady

BY JOEL KAPLAN

My childhood pets were always dogs. Until I lived with Rachel, I had never shared a household with cats.

But after Rachel's father died, her mother was preparing to move to a new home and passed along to us the 16-year-old purebred Maine Coon cat who had been part of the family since Rachel was a teenager. Thus began my introduction to cats.

Cats tend to bring out binary responses in people. Everyone knows how they feel about cats. They either love cats or hate them. But after twenty years, I've come to believe that people who don't like cats really just don't understand them. It has become clear to me that each cat has a unique personality.

Some are aloof; others – many of them – are friendly and passionate. They want to be involved with whatever their people are doing. They become part of your family. Cats are very good judges of character. Recently I accompanied Rachel on a client intervention, as I often do when she's going to a stranger's home. The woman who

had called told us all about how her cat didn't like her boyfriend and how her boyfriend treated the cat. Rachel gave her lots of good advice, but as soon as the door closed behind us, we looked at each other and said, "The boyfriend's gotta go." Sometimes cats just know these things.

Cats are part of Rachel's life in a way that few people can claim. She monitors their moods and their well-being. She insists we avoid disturbing them with noise or movement if they are sleeping. They have the right to half our bed. Sometimes we need to arrange our weekend plans around a cat that needs medication. Our house stays hermetically sealed, with stops on the windows, so that cats can never slip outside. Hiring a cat-sitter if we are leaving town involves an extensive interview process; I like to say it's easier to get into Harvard than to get Rachel's approval as a cat-sitter.

Some of that can be a pain. On the flip side, it's inspiring to see someone who is so passionate about what she does. When people ask me about my wife, I say she's saving the world, one cat at a time. It is truly a labor of love. She doesn't go to sleep at the end of the day until every pending cat problem presented to her has been solved.

Rachel successfully resolved four hundred issues last year for people who would have given their cats to shelters without her help. I'm definitely second fiddle, but that's ok; I'm not that needy.

Recently I was invited to give a talk at a fundraiser for a cat shelter. I stood in front of a room full of cat-lovers and offered this list of "Top 10 signs our cats are loved more than me."

10. The cats never have to clean up their toys.

9. When we go for a ride, Rachel sits in the back with the cats.

8. I'm encouraged not to clean my dinner plate, so the cats can have the leftovers.

7. The heat is on all day for the cats, but when I come home, I have to wear a sweater.

6. I drink water from the tap – the cats choose between sparkling and mineral.

5. If I'm lucky, I get half the bed at night – the cats have beds in every room of the house.

4. Our vet bills are higher than our healthcare bills.

3. I'm not allowed to sneeze around the cats. Did I mention I'm allergic to cats?

2. The ratio of cat pictures to people pictures in our home is 100:1…and I'm not in the 1…

1. And the #1 sign that our cats are loved more than me…when the cats pee and poop around the house, it's considered cute…with me, not so much.

The bottom line is that Rachel understands cats, and if you want to understand your cat, listen to Rachel. I never anticipated becoming a cat person myself, but after more than twenty years, I have to admit, they are a big part of my world now. It's a journey well worth taking.

August 2018
Newton, Massachusetts

CONTENTS

1   How It Began   *1*

2   Sally's Law   *10*

3   Finding My Calling   *18*

4   Let's Make a Deal   *24*

5   What Every Cat Needs   *27*

6   What a Character!   *31*

7   Old Cat, New Cat   *34*

8   Body Language   *50*

9   Can We Talk?   *54*

10   It's Playtime!   *59*

11   I Think We're Alone Now   *63*

12   *Litterbox* Talk   *67*

13   Scratch That   *75*

14   Let's Take It Indoors   *80*

15   We Need to See Other People   *83*

16   It's All In the Training   *86*

17   Calling In Sick   *91*

18   The Hard Work of Saying Goodbye *93*

19   A Particularly Meaningful Success Story   *100*

20   I'm Here for You   *103*

      About the Authors   *111*

❖ *Over the years, my many clients and friends have sent me pictures of their beloved cats, and I have treasured each one. When it came time to illustrate this book, drawing upon this collection of beautiful kitty photos was a natural choice!*

❖ *A portion of the proceeds from sales of this book will directly support my dream of every cat having a loving, forever home.*

This book is dedicated to my Aunt Sally, who shared my love of Tuffy.

SAVING THE WORLD, ONE CAT AT A TIME

~ *1* ~

How It Began

Growing up, I collected cats. First there was Buttercup. Then Dusty, who soon had kittens, of which we kept one. We named that kitten Farfel, and my father, a rabbi, wrote a biblical story for children about my relationship with Farfel. Then Wally came along. Then my music teacher asked for a volunteer to board his cat and I raised my hand. My high school boyfriend Fred gave me Snickers. Later we found Muffin, who stayed with me when I left home and started my adult life.

In short, cats weren't hard to come by in those years. Stray and feral cats populated the fields and forests surrounding our home in the rural farming community of Auburn, Maine. For that matter, so did moose and deer. I'd

By Rachel S. Geller, Ed.D.

take long walks on country roads and see the same feral cats day after day. Once in a while I'd carry one home and say to my parents, "He followed me. Now we have to give him a home!"

Zoe

Today, much of my volunteer work with cats takes place in shelters, where the first thing we do with a stray cat is check for a microchip, then start calling around to other shelters to see if anyone has reported a cat with this description missing. We don't encourage people to just take in cats who follow them home, the way I did as a girl. It was a different time. I lived in a close-knit community; we recognized other families' pets. The cats I took in really had no place else to live.

I like to say that a love for animals was always in my DNA. One summer a cat I took home turned out to be pregnant; I went off to overnight camp as planned, but in every single letter I wrote to my parents, I ended it by saying "Please keep one of the kittens for me!"

SAVING THE WORLD, ONE CAT AT A TIME

I lived with my younger sister and brother and my parents. My younger brother was more of a dog person, so we had two dogs as well, one a Yorkshire terrier given to us by a neighbor who was moving and the other a terrier mix. My sister liked cats, but not as fervently as I did. My parents were generally ambivalent about the animals.

But we had a good household for pets. We lived in a large 150-year-old house with plenty of room, and there weren't many cars around. All the cats were indoor/outdoor animals, which was more widely accepted at that time than it is now. And all the pets got along with one another. We were very much one big happy family.

Even as a girl, I believed that I could communicate with cats in a unique way. I thought about my pets when I was away from them and worried that they were lonely. When I was with them, I'd whisper in their ears and pretend they could understand me. I definitely believed I could understand them.

Pyewacket

3

By Rachel S. Geller, Ed.D.

I think this started with Farfel, the kitten born while I was away at camp. Farfel liked to play in a certain way, and I remember figuring out the rhythm and the nuances that he seemed to respond to best. After that I really felt like we understood each other, like he appreciated my awareness of his needs and preferences.

Although cats are my specific focus at this time in my life, this interest is part of a broader picture. On the larger scale, my passion is helping the vulnerable. Over the years this has manifested in three distinct areas: cats, children with special needs, and the elderly.

Reaching out to those who could use a hand has always been part of my life. The whole time I was growing up, my dad held down two different but concurrent

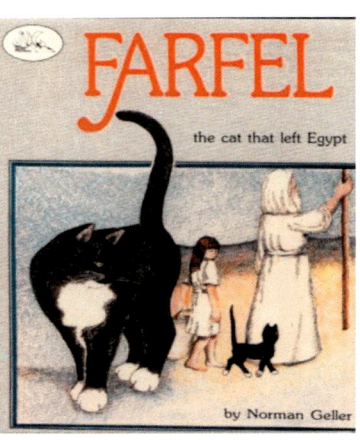

My father, a rabbi, wrote this picture book featuring Farfel and me to illustrate the Exodus of the children of Israel from Egypt.

"I think the kitten likes farfel," Rachel said.

"So do I," answered her mother. "You know, Rachel, the kitten should have a name. We just can't call him kitten all the time."

Rachel thought for a minute and said, "I think we should call him Farfel."

SAVING THE WORLD, ONE CAT AT A TIME

professional roles: he was both a rabbi and a speech pathologist. My summer job during my teenage years was as assistant in his speech therapy practice. That's when I developed my interest in kids with special needs. We had clients with everything from a lisp to Down syndrome. In high school, I signed up to be a peer tutor. At home, as the oldest of three, I babysat my younger siblings and helped out with them whenever I could. My parents joked that I was the only one who understood my brother, who was six years younger than me.

In addition to helping my dad in his speech pathology practice, I helped him in his role as rabbi as well. My father's synagogue included three hundred families. I'd tag along with my father on pastoral calls, helping to comfort people in times of struggle. Because I was good at it, I developed a reputation

Adam

5

By Rachel S. Geller, Ed.D.

as an emotional caregiver. My father was a beloved rabbi known for his intuitive rapport with his congregants, adults and children alike. People saw my skills as a natural auxiliary to his. When one of my friends committed suicide in high school, the principal asked me to deliver the eulogy.

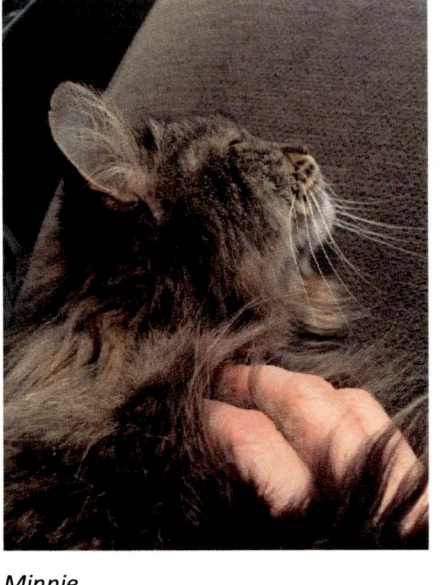

Minnie

As I was finishing high school, I knew I wanted to study either education or psychology. My father's alma mater, Boston University, offered me generous financial aid and promised me a room in one of the brownstones on campus. Given that BU had a fine school of education, I was happy to accept their offer. It turned out to be a very good fit for me. I double-majored in special education and regular education, and minored in psychology.

In the summers, I'd go home to Maine and help in my dad's speech pathology practice, just as I'd done in high school. My father expanded his work to nursing

SAVING THE WORLD, ONE CAT AT A TIME

homes. He'd work with elderly residents who had aphasia as a result of a stroke. As I gained in proficiency working with the elderly patients, my confidence grew as well. My father assigned me one particular patient as a special challenge. I could tell she understood everything I said, but she wouldn't respond to us. One day I was talking with one of the nurses, who mentioned that this woman was quite a musician in her younger years. I had played the piano since

I was five years old and woodwinds since middle school. On a hunch, I brought some instruments to the nursing home and offered them to her. She began playing the instruments, and tears came to her eyes. It was the most interaction

Babka

we'd ever seen from her. My instincts had served me well.

For our student teaching assignments at BU, we drew names of school systems out of a hat. I was randomly placed in the Newton Public Schools and soon fell in love with the community. After graduating from BU, I accepted

7

By Rachel S. Geller, Ed.D.

a full-time position teaching at the Cabot School in Newton. I worked with students who had mild behavioral and emotional special needs.

Shadow

I found a small apartment in Cleveland Circle, a neighborhood in Brookline, and stayed with that job for two years, then entered a master's degree program at Harvard. At that time, computers and technology were just entering the picture in special education, and that was a topic of interest to me. I knew a little bit about programming and wanted to find ways to apply that to teaching special ed students. While attending grad school, I worked part-time at St. Ann's Home, a residential special education program in Methuen.

As it happened, St. Ann's had plans to institute a technology program the following year, so upon graduation I stayed there to implement the new program. After two years in that role, I was running a meeting attended by special needs educators from other communities, one of whom was the director of special needs for the Waltham Public Schools. When I arrived home that same day, I had a

phone message asking if I'd consider working for the Waltham school system. Coincidentally, I'd just gotten married, and my husband Joel and I had bought a condo in Waltham. So I accepted the offer, and stayed with the Waltham Public Schools for the next twenty years.

During that time I worked mostly in the middle schools with the EDBD program – that stands for emotionally disturbed / behaviorally disordered. I covered all the bases in that program: worked directly with students; oversaw testing; wrote up the individualized IEPs; coordinated external services. In 1997 I completed my doctorate in education at BU.

Bandita

By Rachel S. Geller, Ed.D.

~2~

Sally's Law

Sosil (named after my Aunt Sally)

As the story of my early years reflects, I always had a deep sense of compassion – and I always knew how to put my caring sentiments to work, reaching out directly to people and animals in need of help, succor or comfort.

But it was a more recent experience that taught me that sometimes you have to be willing to reach out in a larger capacity. Sometimes it's not enough to provide a helping hand or gentle touch to one person or one

animal – you have to figure out how to use what you know and what you believe in to effect change on a larger scale.

This is why today it's so important to me to work with people on their cat problems. I can't save every cat myself – and Joel would not agree to opening our home to all the cats who need me! My goal through shelters and with individual clients, and now in writing this book, is to spread my knowledge and my expertise as broadly as possible, so that what I know can help as many people and cats as I can possibly reach, not only the ones with whom I come into direct contact.

I learned this lesson not through cats but through family. I found myself in a position where helping one person wasn't enough – I had to find a way to change an entire industry.

Bebe

My father's only sibling was his sister Sally, who was four years his senior. Their parents died when my dad was twelve and Sally was sixteen. Determined to care for her younger brother herself once their parents were gone,

By Rachel S. Geller, Ed.D.

Sally somehow managed to keep their little household of two under the radar, living in an apartment in Dorchester, Massachusetts. Somehow it worked: social services never found out, and on the day Sally turned eighteen, she breathed a big sigh of relief.

Sally was a brilliant woman with a passion for New York Times crossword puzzles, but she put her own life on hold to see my father succeed. He graduated from high school, then college. Finally, once his education was complete, my aunt went back to school herself, earning a degree in social work and eventually becoming a parole officer.

Big Head Cat

Sally had ovarian cancer as a young woman. She survived but it left her unable to have children, and she treated my brother and sister and me as her own. Although she lived in Melrose, Massachusetts, and we were in Maine, we saw her a lot while we were growing up. As the eldest, I was particularly close to her as well as to her husband Sidney. I loved baseball, and when I

SAVING THE WORLD, ONE CAT AT A TIME

visited them they would take me to Red Sox games. Sidney
spent hours practicing pop flies with me.

At barely
seventy, Sally started
to have memory
problems, beyond
the ones that
typically come with
aging. She'd go
places and forget
how to get home.
She had a lot of falls.
And she did things
like leaving the stove
on, putting herself
and her household at
risk. CT scans and brain scans soon revealed that she was
in the early stages of Alzheimer's.

Blackberry

Sidney passed away around that time, and Joel and I
undertook the process of becoming Sally's legal guardians
because we could see what lay ahead for her. When we felt
that she could no longer safely take care of herself, we
hurried to find her a nursing home placement.

By Rachel S. Geller, Ed.D.

The first one we chose didn't have an Alzheimer's unit, so we transferred her elsewhere. The day after we moved her in, I got a call from the nursing home saying she had fallen ill and needed to go to the hospital. I agreed based on their assessment, but when she was examined, the doctors found nothing wrong and said she could go back to the nursing home.

And that was when the nursing home refused to take her back. The nursing home staff told me that she had been screaming all through the night and that they couldn't care for her; moreover, they quoted a law to me saying that they were under no obligation to do so despite that fact that she had already been accepted there.

I became frantic, not knowing what to do about the fact that she suddenly had no place to live. The only option

Moose

I could come up with was having her admitted to the psych ward at a local hospital. What followed was one of the most traumatic events I have ever undergone, seeing my aunt treated in a psych ward. I felt it was unfair and inappropriate to

SAVING THE WORLD, ONE CAT AT A TIME

apply the law about nursing homes not taking people back to Alzheimer's patients. I called my state legislator, Ruth Balser, to say I thought the law needed to be changed. And to my surprise, she called me back the next day and said no such law existed.

I did some research and found out this happens all the time. There's even a name for it within the industry: "dumping." It's when nursing homes take on patients they then realize they can't accommodate so they send the patient to the hospital on some pretext and then won't re-admit them. I wondered how anyone like me, a family member of an elderly person with no prior knowledge of the industry or of nursing home laws, could possibly anticipate this potential happenstance.

But rather than keeping my distress to myself, I took action. An attorney I consulted suggested that I take legal action against the nursing home, but it seemed to me I could spend the rest

Dory

15

By Rachel S. Geller, Ed.D.

of my life mired in an individual lawsuit that wouldn't ultimately help anyone; or I could put that same time and energy into ensuring that no other family would have to undergo the same experience. So instead of suing the nursing home, I put my efforts into changing the law.

I worked with Representative Ruth Balser and her staff to create a nursing home bill of rights, analogous to

Bond

the hospital bill of rights that most of us know about. The nursing home resident or the health proxy receives a copy of the laws pertaining to nursing homes, understands what the patient and family are entitled to, and knows whom to contact if something does not seem right about the patient's care or treatment. And I specified that it had to be written in layperson's language so that anyone could easily grasp it. I even went so far as to specify the font size it had to be published in, to ensure that it could be read by people with diminished vision. Passed in 2010, the law's formal

SAVING THE WORLD, ONE CAT AT A TIME

name is "An Act Protecting Nursing Home Residents," but its nickname is Sally's Law, after my Aunt Sally.

The whole process of writing the bill and getting it passed into law took three years from start to finish. Governor Deval Patrick invited me to a private signing ceremony in recognition of how unusual it was for a private citizen to singlehandedly get a law passed, and he gifted me the pen with which he signed it.

Me with Massachusetts Governor Deval Patrick at the signing of Sally's Law.

By Rachel S. Geller, Ed.D.

~3~

Finding My Calling

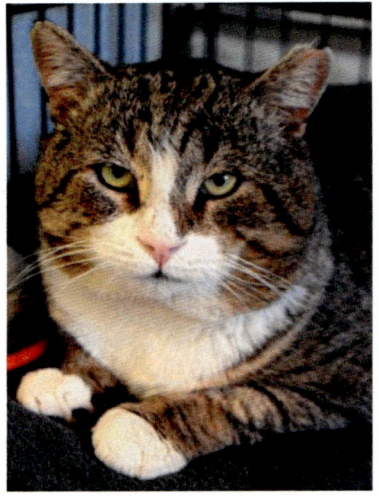

Butch

During the time I was working on Sally's Law, I phased out of classroom teaching and became a private tutor instead. I worked during the afterschool hours with a mix of kids: some who were mainstream and just needed a little extra boost to succeed in school; some who needed help with a specific subject; some who were doing SAT preparation; and some who had special needs like those I'd worked with in the school system. And because tutoring

after school left me with several free hours during the day, I also pursued a long-time goal and started volunteering at animal shelters.

One was the Gifford Cat Shelter in Brighton. Eventually Gifford invited me to serve on their board of directors, which I did for seven years. And I decided to become certified as a cat

Captain Catimer and General Meow

behavior and retention specialist, an official title used by the Humane Society of the United States. The mission of the program is to keep cats in homes so that they don't end up as strays or in shelters. The primary way to do this is to reach out to cat owners who need guidance in solving a problem that might otherwise cause them to get rid of their cat.

One of the requirements for my certification program was to set up a cat behavior and retention program and then document all the cases I saw, the solutions I offered, and the success rates they generated. Since I was on the board at Gifford, that's where I implemented my

BY RACHEL S. GELLER, ED.D.

program. Cats were often brought to Gifford by people who couldn't cope with their pets' behavioral problems. I added an option to the Gifford phone answering system so that one of the options was "For free cat behavior counseling, press 2." The caller would then be forwarded to my cellphone.

People would say to me, "I want to give up my cat because she's peeing on the rug" or some other troublesome behavior. I'd say, "I'll work with you free of charge if you want to keep her." Some people jumped at the opportunity for advice; others had already almost made up their minds to give up their cat by the time they called me. In that case I'd pull at their heartstrings a little. I'd get them to talk a bit about their cat and then I'd say, "I can tell you really love that cat. And I can help you keep her."

Carly

The program I developed had good success rates right away. My first year I had 341 cat behavior cases and successfully resolved 308 of them, meaning that's the number of cats who stayed in

SAVING THE WORLD, ONE CAT AT A TIME

their homes rather than being sent to already overcrowded shelters after their owners consulted with me. When I presented my statistics and client testimonials to the Humane Society, I was asked if my program could be designated as a model program for other shelters to use.

I was invited to serve as a panelist on a Humane Society webinar designed to teach shelters how to institute a cat behavior and retention program. My segment of the webinar was specifically targeted at smaller shelters with limited budgets. That attention opened my eyes to the idea that perhaps this was my calling in life; perhaps I should devote myself even more fully to working on keeping people and their cats together and finding the behavior tactics and techniques that could help that to happen.

Throughout my years of volunteering in shelters, I'd see cute little kittens flying out the door while older cats languished, waiting to be noticed and adopted. Sometimes they had health or behavioral issues. One such cat was Tuffy. He had been abused in the past and so was

Tuffy

By Rachel S. Geller, Ed.D.

not the kind of cat who would run up to you affectionately. Moreover, he had cardiomyopathy. Well, a cat who was standoffish with people and had health issues – I had found my ideal pet.

Soon I decided Tuffy should not be the sole cat in our household. I had heard about two cats who had been trapped from a feral colony in Waltham. They were in a foster home, but no one wanted to adopt them because of their difficult background. When I met them, I noticed how

Minnie and Rosie

cute they were but also observed their behavior and believed I could work with them. I also decided there wasn't too much difference between having two cats and having three. And that's how we ended up with Minnie and Rosie.

Currently I work closely with several cat shelters, training volunteers and offering guidance to people who adopt challenging cats. I also have plans in the works to open a shelter of my own. In the spring of 2018, the Boston Globe did a feature on my work with cats, and

SAVING THE WORLD, ONE CAT AT A TIME

that brought in a deluge of emails from people across the country and even in Canada wanting advice on how to deal with their cats. Clients had long told me that I should write a book about cat behavior, and the Globe story seemed like a sign that the time had come.

So this book is my attempt to consolidate my years of experience with cats and their owners in order to help even more cat owners who feel challenged by their pet's behavior. Or maybe I can even reach readers who don't have these problems and can use my techniques to ensure they never do. In the following pages I've compiled the questions I am most typically asked and the answers that seem to work.

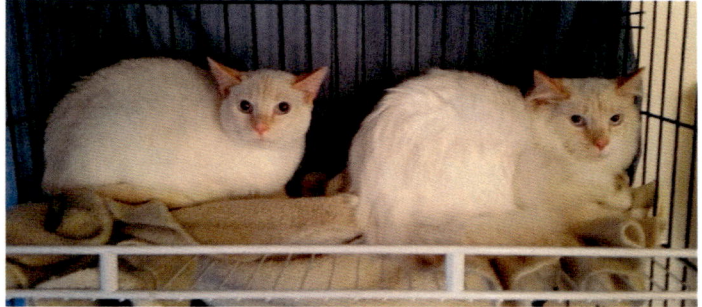

Casper and Polar Bear

By Rachel S. Geller, Ed.D.

~4~

Let's Make a Deal

Recently a woman called me who had just finished the process of adopting a cat from a shelter but hadn't brought the cat home yet. She already had a cat at home and wanted advice on how to introduce the new cat to the

resident cat, and I was delighted to hear from her at this stage.

Talking with a client about introducing a new cat before the new cat comes home is the perfect scenario because I can help the client get everything set up and head

Ceci

24

SAVING THE WORLD, ONE CAT AT A TIME

off any potential problems at the pass. Understandably, most people don't call me until they have a problem, when the cats are already together. So I laid out a whole program for her, detailing all the steps I recommend for introducing two cats.

A week later she called me again. I was happy to hear from her and eager for an update. To my surprise, she said, "Things aren't going well at all. The cats hate each other."

Charcoal

This was puzzling to me because if she had been following the program we set out, she couldn't possibly know that yet because the cats wouldn't even have officially met. The program we designed would have taken three or four weeks in total before its success could be evaluated.

I wanted to deduce where it went wrong. "How was the scent-swapping phase?" I asked. That's one of the first steps.

25

By Rachel S. Geller, Ed.D.

"Oh, we skipped that part," she replied. "My old cat's smells are already all over the house, so we didn't think it was important to go through that stage."

I was steaming. That's an important step! But she skipped it, and now the two cats hated each other. This was going to be really difficult to fix, not to mention that the cat owner was now discouraged and doubting that it could possibly work between these two cats. That meant the new cat might lose her home and be returned to the shelter – all because the owner didn't bother to follow the advice I gave.

I tell this story to urge people to give my methods a chance. If you are willing to admit that something is a

 problem for your pets, or at the very least a challenge, and you're willing to ask my advice or take the time to read what I have to say about it, I implore you to also follow the steps I set out for each kind of problem. Don't skip anything. Just give this a chance.

Charlotte

SAVING THE WORLD, ONE CAT AT A TIME

~5~

What Every Cat Needs

I'm about to bring home my first cat. What do I need to buy or acquire to make my new pet feel at home?

1. **Litterboxes**. My rule of thumb is that you should have one more litterbox than the number of cats in the household, and the litterboxes should be stationed throughout your home in various rooms. This gives your cat plenty of options and the chance to feel in control.

Checkers

   Cats feel vulnerable in litterboxes. If you have more than one, you increase your odds of their

27

successful use by placing them in locations your cat likes. Moreover, some cats don't want to pee and poop in the same box, so it's good to have two boxes even for just one cat. I understand that litterboxes are not the most pleasant accessory of cathood, and some people don't like the idea of litterboxes all over the house, but I tell my clients it's better than cats having accidents.

2. **Scratching posts.** Have one scratching post per cat as well. They like their own scent on the post they use. I've included more detail about scratching posts in Chapter 13, but the important features of a good scratching post are sisal- or rope-wrapped; at least three feet tall; and sturdy, not wobbly.

3. **Food and water bowls.** I do think it's a good idea to

have more than one feeding station in your house, especially if you have more than one cat. Some cats will share their bowl with other cats; others like to have their own. So, to be safe, especially if you are introducing a new cat to the household, it's

Cinder

SAVING THE WORLD, ONE CAT AT A TIME

prudent to have a feeding station for each cat. Another plus is that if something happens to the food – such as if it gets spilled – there is another option for the cat. I would suggest the same for water; having one more water bowl than cats is always a good idea, and if water gets spilled or dirty, your cats always have other bowls from which to drink.

4. **Cat toys.** I divide cat toys into two categories: solo and interactive. Solo toys are for when you are out and have left your cat at home alone;

Minnie

interactive toys are toys such as fishing poles that you and your cat can use to play together. Have at least a few toys per cat, and replenish them once in a while. If you've noticed that your cat has been ignoring a particular toy, put it away for a while and introduce a new toy. Then swap out the old one later and see if it now seems more interesting.

5. **Cat trees or perches.** Cats live in a more vertical world than we do because they can jump five times

BY RACHEL S. GELLER, ED.D.

their height. Vertical space is important to cats, and cat trees or perches are a way for them to safely exploit their attraction to heights. A perch can be an actual pet item designed specifically for this purpose, or it can be as simple as a towel folded on a bureau top. There are two reasons to create vantage points of various heights at locations you've selected for your cat. In a multi-cat household, tiered vertical spaces allow cats to express their hierarchy, claim their territory and establish some personal space, if they wish to do so. Even if you have just one cat, a comfortable perch at some height off the ground, especially near a window, will give him a

vantage point from which to observe the passing scene, something that helps to keep a cat's mind busy.

Felicia and Magnum

SAVING THE WORLD, ONE CAT AT A TIME

~6~

What a Character!

I know just what I'm looking for in a pet. Will I be able to find a cat at the shelter whose personality matches my criteria?

Choosing a cat from the shelter based on the cat's personality can be tricky. Surrounded by other cats and random volunteers, new to the environment, quite likely anxious and intimidated, a cat may show a very different personality at the shelter than he or she will show once established in a safe and comfortable home. Many people

Duffy

31

By Rachel S. Geller, Ed.D.

want to find a cat who will walk right up to them and seek affection, but sometimes various factors in the shelter environment mean that just won't happen. I urge visitors to take a chance on a shy or quiet cat who will change once trust is established.

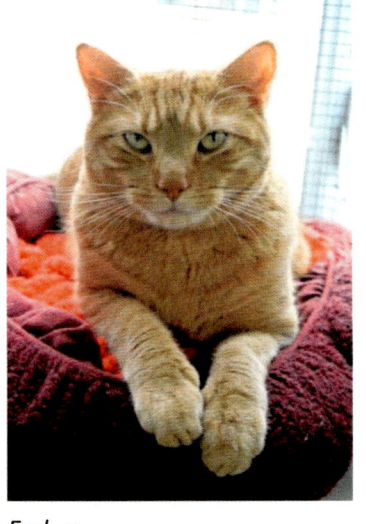

Ember

I've seen cats at the shelter who seem terrified and don't want to be touched by anyone. Someone will adopt the cat, bring him home, and a week later send me a photo of the cat lying on his back enjoying a tummy rub. Cats who might seem shy and withdrawn at the shelter may blossom into affectionate extroverts once they are brought home. So when visitors to the shelter ask me to help them select a cat based on the traits they are looking for, it's not always a sure thing that I'll be able to meet their criteria.

It is also worth noting that cats have fluid personalities until they go through social maturity, which happens between the ages of two and four. Once a cat is four years old, what you see is what you get: the cat is

SAVING THE WORLD, ONE CAT AT A TIME

unlikely to undergo further changes in behavior or personality unless there is a major alteration to the cat's environment. So that's a major benefit of adopting a slightly older cat!

Hero

By Rachel S. Geller, Ed.D.

~7~

Old Cat, New Cat

I am a long-time owner of one cat but would like to add a second cat to the household. How do I make this process go smoothly?

Everyone I work with at the Cat Connection knows how I, a Maine native, love Maine Coon cats. So when one arrived at the shelter recently, I immediately got a phone

 call from a colleague. An elderly woman was moving to a new home that didn't allow pets, and she was going to have to give up her Maine Coon cat. Would I consider

Loverboy and Rosie

SAVING THE WORLD, ONE CAT AT A TIME

taking her myself, my colleagues asked, rather than seeing her stay at the shelter?

It was an emotional time for me. I was mourning two wonderful cats who passed away within a few months of each other. I didn't think I had the bandwidth to take on a new cat right then. Introducing a new cat to the household is a big deal. It's like bringing a new person into your household. You have to introduce everyone and let them get to know each other. You can't expect one big happy family right away.

I told my colleagues I'd think about it, expecting to decide in the end that I needed more time to get over my

recent losses. But instead, what I found myself thinking was, Here's a cat who needs a home. And that's what my work is dedicated to: putting cats in homes rather than shelters. Here's a cat who might like to be in my home.

Sosil

35

By Rachel S. Geller, Ed.D.

I was wrong to think I didn't have the bandwidth, I realized. The two recent deaths had left my heart not closed off to more animals but open and full of love, ready to take on a creature who needed me. And this cat needed me.

Clients very often seek advice on how to successfully bring a new cat into a household that already has a resident cat. Now it was time to take my own best advice.

I named my new cat Sosil, after my beloved Aunt Sally – Sosil is the Yiddish form of Sally. When I brought her home, I knew the first step was to let Sosil be alone for two or three days to become acclimated to the household. Clients are sometimes surprised when I instruct them to put a new cat in isolation – they think the cat will be lonely. But it actually allows the cat to develop confidence and a sense of security in a new place.

Elijah

Meanwhile, my long-time cat Elijah could sense that there was another cat nearby and could start becoming accustomed to the idea. He could hear Sosil meowing, moving around, and eating. But

SAVING THE WORLD, ONE CAT AT A TIME

he had no reason to feel threatened because the cat was not in his space. So he was becoming curious without developing any negative feelings about her.

I gave Sosil her own room for about a week, and then very gradually began a structured introduction process. In that time, she learned that she could trust these new people in this new home. We fed her, watered her, played with her and kept her company, so that she got the message that we were here to provide for her and take care of her.

Before you bring home your new cat, choose a room the cat can inhabit alone for a few days. I call it the sanctuary room. In the sanctuary room, put food and water bowls, a litter box, a scratching post, and some toys. A small room is best, ideally without furniture that they can hide beneath: a room in which they will feel safe out in the open.

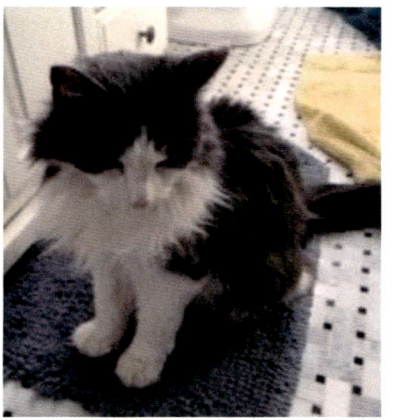

Sheldon

When you first bring your new cat home, take the cat carrier with the cat in it right away to the sanctuary room. Open the door of the carrier, close the door of the

37

room, and walk away. The cat will emerge from the carrier as soon as he feels safe. There's no hurry.

Nellie

Once you've established the new cat in the sanctuary room, your resident cat is going to know that there's another animal in the house. She will smell and hear this new animal. If the resident cat acts perturbed, scratching at the door or meowing a lot, try to distract her. Play with her, soothe her, gently lead her away from the door if she's scratching at it, but try to act like it's no big deal. If you get anxious, the cat is going to pick up on it and think the newcomer is cause for anxiety. Be present for your resident cat, but act like life is just going on as usual.

Additionally, leave an oversized shirt in the sanctuary room for yourself to put on over your clothes when you go in to feed or play with your new cat. Wash your hands before you go into the sanctuary room as well. This isn't a drastic measure, but it will somewhat mute the scents of the resident cat and won't give the new cat quite

SAVING THE WORLD, ONE CAT AT A TIME

as much sensory stimulus to try to organize. It also prevents your resident cat from being too overwhelmed by new cat smells on you.

Maintain the sanctuary room as a private space for your newcomer for three or four days. By around that time, you should start to sense that your newcomer is calming

down and becoming comfortable with his new surroundings. In Sosil's case, although there was some hissing and growling when I first brought her home, after about three days she showed some obvious changes in behavior that demonstrated she was becoming increasingly content. She

Grady

ran up to me when I entered the sanctuary room. She was eating and drinking and using the litterbox. She was happy to have me pet her. Taken together, these were signs that she was ready for the next step of integration, which I call the scent communication phase.

BY RACHEL S. GELLER, ED.D.

For the scent communication phase, take a sock and rub your resident cat around the face, ears and neck with it. Then leave that sock in the sanctuary room. Do the same using another sock with the new cat, and place that sock wherever the resident cat likes to spend time.

Throughout the introduction process, maintain the mindset that the resident cat has control over the situation and everything gets her approval before you move on to anything else. Put the scented sock somewhere in her space, but don't push her to examine it. Let her gather information on her own schedule. Repeat the process of rubbing the respective sock on each cat a few times throughout the day to keep the scent fresh. Monitor each cat's reaction. Soon they should seem accustomed to the new smell and not perturbed by it.

The next step in the scent communication phase is a soil swap, which is just what it sounds like. Move a small

 sample of soiled litter from each cat into the other cat's litterbox. This continues the process of getting them familiar with

Frostie

SAVING THE WORLD, ONE CAT AT A TIME

each other's scents before they meet in person. Again, watch for promising signs such as calm behavior, normal eating and drinking, and unagitated litterbox use to suggest that they accept the new scent.

Now it's time for the visual introduction. Open the door to the sanctuary room just a crack. Give each cat some food, water and toys in his own space with a good distance between them. They can eat, drink and play within their comfort zone, and they can start peeking out at the other cat when they are ready. Keep the visual introduction sessions short and end on a positive note. Even if they haven't been looking at each other through the door, they're still aware of the other's presence. After a few minutes, close the door to the sanctuary room again until next time.

Goldie and Liza

Continue the visual introduction phase by repeating that process once or twice a day over the next few days, but each time open the door to the sanctuary room a few inches more and move the food bowls a little bit closer. The goal is to have them eating in each other's presence – that's a very good sign that they are feeling secure. You might hear

By Rachel S. Geller, Ed.D.

Oreo and Achilles

an occasional hiss between them, which is no reason to panic. It's a natural sign of defensiveness. What you don't want to hear is growling, which is aggressive. If there's any growling, slow down the process and just continue opening the door a crack for a few minutes, a few times a day.

Once you've reached this point successfully and the two cats are eating in each other's presence, give your resident cat a few minutes of confinement while you allow the new cat to explore the house on her own. This serves two purposes. It enables the newcomer to gather information about her new environment, and it also allows her to deposit her own scent throughout the house so that the resident cat will begin to understand that this new cat will eventually be in all the same places that she tends to be herself. Let that go on for about fifteen minutes; then put the newcomer back in the sanctuary room and release the resident cat from confinement. The following day, repeat

this process twice for about twenty minutes each time. On the third day, try three sessions of up to forty-five minutes.

When that stage is complete, put two baby gates, one on top of the other, in the doorway to the sanctuary room separating the cats. Feed and play with each of them separately while they

Elijah and Rosie

have full visibility of each other. Do this for a few days. As long as there is no growling, it's finally time to let them meet one another without any impediments. Leave an opening in the baby gates that they can pass through but still retreat behind if one needs an escape. Stay with them and watch carefully to be sure they are getting along. They don't have to play together or make contact; they just need to tolerate one another and not show any aggression.

This last stage can take from two to four weeks, which may seem like a long time when you just want to treat them like equals and friends, but it will be well worth the time you've spent when the result is cats that get along.

By Rachel S. Geller, Ed.D.

The biggest mistake you can make is to rush the process and then find yourself with two fighting cats.

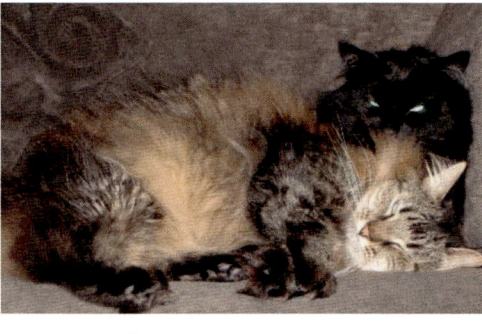

Minnie and Rosie

This method actually works if you are introducing a cat to a dog as well. You might have to crate the dog when they are becoming accustomed to each other's presence, because letting the dog run after the cat would definitely get things off on the wrong foot. Go at the cat's pace, letting her take the lead. Play with each animal separately, letting the other see. Remember that cats are territorial. In becoming accustomed to a dog, your cat needs to know first of all the she is safe and secondly that the dog isn't going to overtake her territory. Ultimately, by taking your time introducing your two cats and making each one comfortable with the situation, you've created something better than what you started out with: a two-cat household.

Two cats are the right choice for a lot of people because the cats have company, but the number isn't overwhelming for the cat owner. Many cats like to have a

SAVING THE WORLD, ONE CAT AT A TIME

friend. So if you are just starting out as a cat owner, the way to bypass all of this effort is to adopt two together. Littermates are ideal because they are likely to be bonded already, but if no littermates are available at the shelter you visit, just ask the staff there which cats get along with each other.

I've known a few cats in my lifetime who did not like any other cats, but most have the ability to get along, though there's a wide spectrum of ways this gets expressed. Some cats play together

George

and snuggle up together; others merely tolerate one another's presence. This doesn't correlate to size or gender. I have had many clients tell me that their smallest cat is the one in charge! It's really just a matter of personality and attitude.

Another good tip about choosing a new cat if you already have one or more at home is to select a cat who is at least four years old. Cats go through social maturity between two and four years old. That means up to age four,

BY RACHEL S. GELLER, ED.D.

they might still change a lot; but if a cat is four or older, the personality he shows you is the personality he is likely to demonstrate forever.

Jacoby

There are even rare cases where a cat who goes through social maturity changes in regard to how well he gets along with other cats. He might become more dominant or aggressive at that point. Sometimes you have to do an actual reintroduction process as if the cats have never met. If you do that, the cat who has become more aggressive should be treated like the newcomer and put in the sanctuary room. You want to give the aggressive cat less prime real estate within the house and not reward him for his new behavior. Go through the same steps I outlined for introducing a new cat, and don't expect it to go any faster. Watch closely for signs of fighting, and confine the aggressor cat in the sanctuary room if you see that happen.

Cats are by nature hierarchical. It is the very rare multi-cat household that does not have a pecking order.

SAVING THE WORLD, ONE CAT AT A TIME

Therefore, your goal should not be to have cats that are perpetually harmonious and egalitarian but rather to make it easy for them to express their hierarchy without fighting, intimidation or posturing.

One easy way to do this is by using vertical space to your advantage. We humans tend to occupy space in a horizontal way as we walk from one point to another, but a cat's world is vertical. For them, hierarchy is not only an abstraction – it manifests literally. The most dominant or alpha cat takes the highest perch.

You can make this particularly easy for them by providing them with cat trees. Or you can simply create places that will be comfortable for them to perch, such as a bookshelf or dresser with a cat bed placed on top. When I visit a client whose cats are not getting along, one of the first things I look at is whether there are various tiered spaces that the cats can use to assert their dominance.

Of course, when I suggest cat trees – as well as scratching posts, cat beds on

Elijah

47

BY RACHEL S. GELLER, ED.D.

shelves, or special toys – some people are automatically opposed to my suggestion because they don't believe they should have to spend money to accommodate their cats' behavior. And sometimes it's not the money but just the idea that they should have to change their own décor or style or behavior to accommodate a cat. When that's the case, I try to focus on easy fixes, like a towel on a dresser top for a cat who needs a higher space.

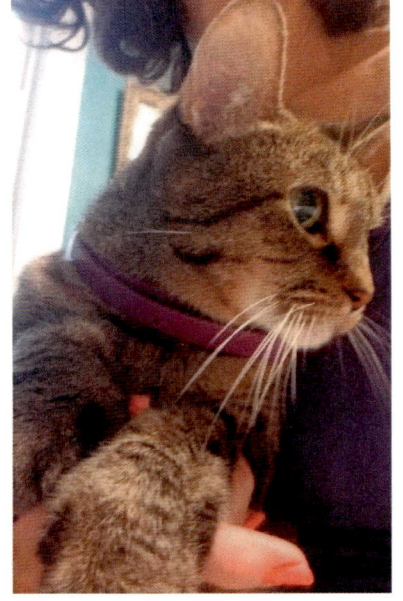

Ginger

It is worth remembering that feral cats live in colonies. People have developed something of a myth about cats' independence. Maybe cats act independent from people compared to dogs, but the reality is that they are group animals. They live in groups that include leaders and followers. They may be solitary hunters, but they are not independent beings. This is why they typically do sociable things like greet you at the door and follow you around the house, though for some reason people whose

SAVING THE WORLD, ONE CAT AT A TIME

cats do those typical things often seem to think their cat is rare in those practices. Facilitating ways to create little societies within your household – whether it's with two or more cats, a mixture of cats and dogs, or if necessary just one cat with one or two people who are very engaged with the cat – will help to ensure that you have happy pets.

Harry

By Rachel S. Geller, Ed.D.

~8~

Body Language

I've heard conflicting explanations of how to read my cat's cues when it comes to things like tail twitching. What can I learn from watching my cat?

Huffletuff and Tews

When I do training sessions with shelter volunteers, we talk a lot about cats' body language. The first thing to understand in trying to read your cat's moods and feelings through his body language is that 90 percent of what cats are trying to tell you boils down to one of two sentences: "Come

closer" or "Stay away." Cats' attitudes about people mostly have to do with wanting the distance between themselves and the human to either increase or decrease. And quite a lot of the time, you can tell which message they are trying to convey merely by looking at their tails or ears.

Cats rely heavily on their tails to communicate their mood. This is an interesting evolutionary relic, hearkening back to when cats lived outside in grasslands and jungles. Tails are easy for other cats to spot from a distance, over the tall grass or the brush.

A cat whose tail is pointing straight up is communicating that she is happy and content and feeling approachable. He is confident and not afraid. A horizontal tail on a cat who is walking is also a sign that the cat is in a good frame of mind. Maybe wary, but

Jonah

not anxious. Essentially, a tail positioned anywhere from 90 to 180 degrees from the cat's back shows that the animal is

BY RACHEL S. GELLER, ED.D.

Hope

feeling fine. On the other hand, if a cat's tail is angled down, it might be a sign of fear or aggression.

It's important to recognize that from a body language perspective, cats are the opposite of dogs when it comes to tails. A happy dog wags her tail faster and faster. The opposite is true for cats; their tails twitch and lash when they are agitated, and the faster the tail moves, the more anxious the cat feels. A cat gently swishing his tail might be feeling fine, but lashing back and forth is a sign that the cat wants to be left alone.

Think of a tail straight up as a green light to approach, a tail angled down as a yellow light, and a switching or lashing tail as a red light. And when a cat wraps its tail around your arm or your body, or around himself, that's a sign of trust.

Ears are another interesting cue. If a cat's ears are pointing straight up, he is feeling calm, engaged, curious and happy. If his ears are making a T from his head, like airplane wings, that's a sign of fear. And the time you

SAVING THE WORLD, ONE CAT AT A TIME

should most leave a cat alone is when he is rotating his ears back and down. That's a sign of aggression. Physically it means he is protecting his eardrums in preparation for going into battle.

People sometimes complain to me that their cat bit or scratched them with no warning. I tend to think there probably was a warning; the victim just didn't know how to read it. Understanding tail and ear position will take you a long way toward understanding your cat.

Isaac

By Rachel S. Geller, Ed.D.

~9~

Can We Talk?

My cats purr, meow, growl, and hiss….but how do I interpret their many different ways of vocalizing?

After body language, the next best way for you to understand your cat is to decode his vocalization. Cats are unusual in that very few other non-human creatures vocalize sounds of contentment. Throughout nearly all of the mammalian animal kingdom, noises that animals

Jack

intentionally make – barking, mooing, whinnying, oinking, squeaking – express something other than a state of serenity, such as anxiety or want.

54

Saving the World, One Cat at a Time

Cats meow and purr when they are comfortable and happy. Moreover, meowing is in fact a form of communication that evolved specifically in relation to humans. Cats don't meow to each other. The sounds they direct toward each other are hissing or growling, both to show defensiveness or aggression.

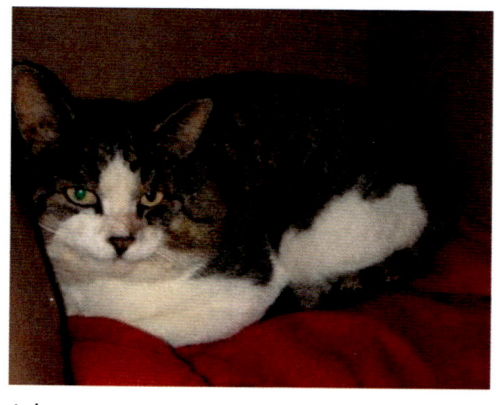

Jake

Cats not only meow for us people; they learn to adapt their meowing to our reactions. They change intonation and pitch. Your cat might have one meow for hunger, another for distress or anxiety, another as a greeting. Respond appropriately every time and you will develop a very compatible communication style with your cat.

Cats purr when they are happy, but they also purr to soothe themselves. When I bring my cat to the vet, she purrs: not because she's happy but because the purring vibration helps her to calm herself.

This can lead to confusion. I talk to clients who are puzzled because their new cat was purring when they

By Rachel S. Geller, Ed.D.

brought her home but then suddenly she scratched. When I hear that, I'll quiz the client on what else was going on with the cat. Usually I'll learn that the cat was lashing her tail or holding her ears flat, but the new owner believed that the purring meant all was well. In reality the cat was terrified and was using all kinds of repetitive messaging to say so, while purring to soothe her own fears, but the owner wasn't getting the message. The cat finally felt like she had no other choice than to bite or scratch because the person wasn't listening.

So if the cat is purring, look at other cues. Cat behavior doesn't occur in a vacuum. Look at the environment and assess what's going on.

A new cat might hiss when he first comes home. Clients tell me that their new cat doesn't like them and behaves aggressively toward them, but I explain that the cat is afraid and is just trying to cope.

Jewel

SAVING THE WORLD, ONE CAT AT A TIME

If you are met with hissing or any other sign of aggression, it's important to gradually desensitize the cat to your presence. Walk slowly toward your new cat, stopping at whatever point she starts to respond negatively, with hissing or tail switching. And then stay right there. Hang out. Sit on the floor. Take out your phone and check your email. Don't pay attention to the cat. By focusing elsewhere, you come across as non-threatening.

Leah

When the cat's aggressive behavior ceases, move gradually in very small increments, inch by inch, closer. When the cat hisses, stop, and again, just stay where you are for a while. Remember, the cat doesn't know this is a loving home where she is wanted. She just sees someone expecting to touch her. Create a bond by finding that starting point where the cat will accept you and slowly, conservatively, move closer to the cat.

Food can be very motivating also. Offer your cat some tuna on the end of a spoon as you are slowly

acclimating her to your presence, and she will come to associate you with safety and comfort.

Work on this in a 15-minute session, once or twice a day, and leave the cat alone the rest of the time. Gradually lengthen the duration of the sessions and increase their number throughout the day. Eventually you will earn your cat's trust.

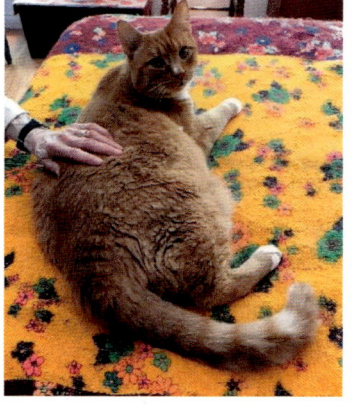
Jigs

To recap, when you are trying to gauge your cat's mood, bear in mind that meowing and purring means he is engaging with you, usually in a positive way. A tail or ears held up are also a good sign that your cat is feeling confident, alert and comfortable with the situation. If you see tail or ears pointing sideways or down, or a lashing tail; if you hear hissing or growling; all of those are signs that it's time to figure out what the problem is and how you can help it to get solved for your cat.

SAVING THE WORLD, ONE CAT AT A TIME

~10~

It's Playtime!

A lot of people don't really know how cats like to play. When I tell clients I'm going to teach them to play with their cats, I see their eyes glaze over and I know what they're thinking: How hard can it be to play with some toys?

Simba

But there's a technique, and if you understand how to play with your cat the way cats like, you'll reap the rewards of a happy, stimulated, non-anxious cat with whom you can spend quality time.

What I frequently see is someone pick up a toy and wave it in a cat's face to try to engage the cat's interest. That puts the cat in a defensive mode. More importantly, it

59

By Rachel S. Geller, Ed.D.

Lindsay

doesn't bear any resemblance to a real-life situation. What cats like best is play that simulates hunting, and there is no prey that jumps around in a cat's face. Hunting and catching prey are what make them feel engaged, curious and confident. So whenever you are playing, think about whether you are replicating the hunting experience for them.

The very best interactive toy for you and your cat to play with together is a fishing pole type of toy. That puts both of you in the game together. For a shy cat or one just getting to know you, the pole creates a comfort zone, a boundary. A big part of the game is to act like prey. Think of how prey would act. Using whatever is at the end of the fishing pole toy, fly it around; slither it across the floor; make it hop like a frog. All of these actions will stimulate your cat's prey drive and put him in hunter mode. For cats, hunter mode is like long-distance running for some humans: it releases endorphins and feel-good chemicals.

SAVING THE WORLD, ONE CAT AT A TIME

Some people make the mistake of thinking the goal when playing with a cat is to keep the toy away from the cat. But if you keep in

Monroe and Rosalee

mind that play should simulate hunting, you can see how that just creates immeasurable frustration. For the cat, the most important part of the game is the capture. They want the physical, tangible sense of success that comes from watching, stalking, pouncing and ultimately catching. That's what makes the cat feel empowered. So as you play with the fishing pole toy, be sure that many times throughout the game the cat actually captures the object. That creates good feelings and positive associations for him. It releases anxiety and tension.

What really bothers me is to see people playing with their cats using laser pointers. People think it's amusing to watch cats chase a point of light, but if you understand that cats love the act of hunting, it will be obvious that nothing could be more frustrating – and ultimately anxiety-provoking – to a cat than trying to catch

BY RACHEL S. GELLER, ED.D.

an intangible speck of light. Laser pointers are for PowerPoint presentations, not for cat play.

Stay with the game for a while. Intersperse the chasing and pouncing with plenty of captures. Finish the game with one last successful capture. To make it a perfect play experience, let the climax of the game happen when you give the cat a little treat that simulates the feasting after a hunt.

Felicia

SAVING THE WORLD, ONE CAT AT A TIME

~11~

I Think We're Alone Now

Is it true that cats are fine when left alone? Is there a length of time after which my cat will become lonely or bored?

Despite their reputation as solitary creatures, many cats suffer from separation anxiety when their owners are out of the house, whether it's for a long day of work or a long weekend out of town. Worrying about how your cat will manage when you're away shouldn't keep you from

what you need or want to do away from home – nor should it keep you from adopting a cat.

The key to resolving your cat's separation anxiety is to help build her confidence. Start with interactive play, involving several captures, as I've described in the previous chapter. That helps your cat build overall confidence. Next you want the cat to feel confident when alone. Again, toys are your best tool – in this case solitary toys like puzzle feeders. That's an octagon-shaped ball that cats can bat and

Maggie

roll around; once in a while a snack rolls out. Little catnip toys are fun for solo play also. Of course, your cat will spend a lot of time in your absence napping or lolling, so provide blankets or cat beds for that purpose. Give your cat ways to occupy her brain and her body while you are gone. The more she feels stimulated by toys, games and challenges, the less she will notice your absence.

Anything you can do to make the environment feel familiar, such as background noise and light, will also

SAVING THE WORLD, ONE CAT AT A TIME

mitigate your cat's anxiety. Leaving on a TV or radio and a few lights will help make the cat less aware of being alone.

Also, avoid the temptation to make a huge fuss over your pet when you return. Too much activity and attention directed toward your cat when you reenter the household can just serve to increase the tension of the situation. Maintain normalcy, so that the reunion feels calm rather than overstimulating to your cat.

Little Tyke

Most cats are not enthusiastic travelers, because they don't like change. If you have a vacation house you visit often, you can probably get your cat accustomed to it through regular visits, but if you are going someplace new, leave your cat at home. They like their own spaces, routines, smells, and a general sense of familiarity.

Most cats can be left alone in their homes with a responsible, experienced pet sitter when their owners go out of town or take a vacation. The pet sitter can be a

BY RACHEL S. GELLER, ED.D.

professional, but many times the pet sitter is a family member or close friend who knows the cat. I believe that it's not only acceptable but beneficial for cats to be allowed to stay home in their familiar environment when you are traveling. If you'll be going away for a week, acclimate your cat to the idea by starting with a few weekends with the cat sitter first, so that your cat becomes familiar with this new person's presence.

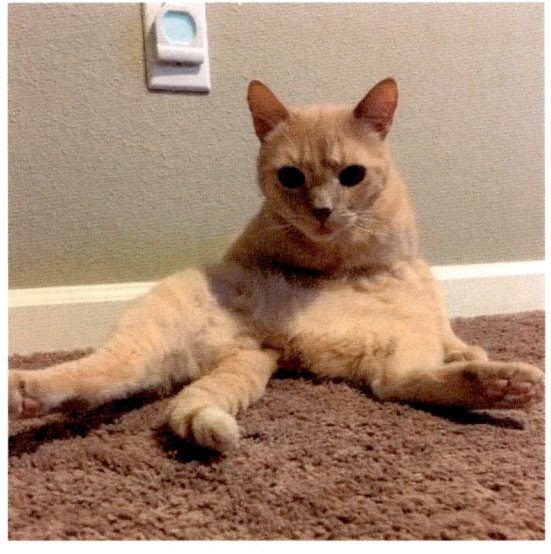

Stanley

SAVING THE WORLD, ONE CAT AT A TIME

~*12*~

Litterbox Talk

Help! My cat won't use the litterbox!

A huge majority of panicked questions I get concern litterbox use. Some cats will use their litterbox sometimes but not all the time; in other cases I hear from people who have just brought a new cat home and can't get the cat to use the litterbox at all.

Sarah

I start the discussion by running through a series of questions. Where is the litterbox located? What is its

67

configuration? One common mistake my clients make is to go overboard with the concept of privacy. They assume that the more secluded and private they can make the litterbox, the more comfortable the cat will be using it.

Lacey

But they are wrong. Privacy is generally more of a human construct than a concept for cats. People think they are creating the perfect bathroom environment by putting the litterbox in a secluded part of the house, in a dark corner. But in reality, if a cat has to go on a hike and an archaeological dig to find the litterbox, he will give up and not use it at all.

Of course, there's another reason that humans put litterboxes far from view. Thinking their cats want privacy may be one motivator, but the other is simply the issue of palatability: people don't want to have to see and smell the litterbox in their own primary living spaces.

I remind them that having a litterbox in the living room or near the kitchen may not seem particularly appealing, but surely it's better than pee or poop accidents

SAVING THE WORLD, ONE CAT AT A TIME

all over the house. You might just have to take a deep breath and overcome your own aversion to the litterbox's presence in order to have it somewhere in which your cat will feel comfortable using it.

Cats not only want easy accessibility to their litterbox; they want to feel safe once they are in it. That means clear lines of sight. If you tuck the litterbox into a corner, your cat might feel – well, cornered. Cats are sensitive to vulnerability. They are always aware of opponents, real or imagined. Even if your cat is the only one in the household, she will be constantly attuned to the possible presence of invaders.

When I go to a client's house to help with a litterbox problem, I first ask to see where they keep the litterbox. Bathrooms are popular places, particularly wedged between the toilet and the wall. Again, it may look safe and private to you, but to a cat it feels like a place of vulnerability. I tell clients to think like a cat. If you were in this spot, could you see

Walter

BY RACHEL S. GELLER, ED.D.

Sassy

around the corner; could you see out the door? Or do you think you might feel cornered or trapped?

Sometimes it's as easy as pulling the litterbox away from the wall or out of the corner. Sometimes the answer is to put the litterbox closer to the door, so the cat can see into the hallway. When I consult in a litterbox problem, I try to imagine it from the cat's perspective. If I were using the litterbox there, what could I see and what could I not see?

If you think location might indeed be the problem, try putting the litterbox in the middle of a room, just to see if the cat will then use it. If he does, move it just a couple of inches per day back to where you want it. Of course, if the box eventually reaches a spot where for whatever reason the cat will no longer use it, you might need to compromise on what you consider the ideal location.

Suppose your litterbox is in an open, easily accessible area and meets all my criteria for a good location. But your cat still won't use it. What could the problem be?

SAVING THE WORLD, ONE CAT AT A TIME

Once again, adopt the perspective of a cat, and this time consider the litter itself. Is it scented? If so, your cat might be bothered by the smell. Anything that seems artificial to them is going to raise their anxiety. Look for a litter that replicates a place they might choose to go to the bathroom outdoors – most likely by being unscented, and also soft and sandy.

What about visual cues in the litterbox? We've already talked about not having its location be too secluded or cornered. But a similar problem is litterboxes with covers. Like hiding the litterbox away, people do this to meet their own aesthetic preference – in this case not having to look into the

Lucia

litterbox. But again, cats take comfort in being out in the open. A litterbox with a concealing cover will make them feel anxious and vulnerable just the way a cornered location will.

Not long ago I was called to a client's house to advise him on why his new cat wasn't using the litterbox. I

71

BY RACHEL S. GELLER, ED.D.

asked to see the litterbox location. Not only was it down a long hall and up a flight of stairs, but there was a more dominant resident cat who liked to hide in that hallway. The new cat was afraid to pass down that hallway to reach his litterbox because it meant encroaching on another cat's territory. To me it seemed obvious, but the client simply hadn't thought about that.

Another factor: noise. Some people like to put litterboxes in laundry rooms for the same reason they like bathrooms: laundry rooms tend to be tucked away well out of sight and are almost never visited by guests to the home. Again, take on your cat's perspective. What are laundry rooms often full of? Noise. Washing machines and dryers spin, whir, click, thump and sometimes buzz. All of this noise could be reason alone for the cat not to want to go into this room.

Is the size of the box right? You might have been

Mitzi

using the same litterbox since your cat was a kitten, and he may have simply outgrown it. Conversely, a very old cat might find it hard to step over a lip at the edge of the box. Look for any possible reasons

related to the box's physical structure that might cause the cat to reject it.

Finally, as with any behavioral issue with animals, rule out any possible medical factors. See the vet to ensure that your cat doesn't have a urinary tract infection or a kidney

Peanuts

problem. Because if he associates the litterbox with physical pain, then of course he's not going to use it.

I encourage my clients to play with their cats near the litterbox. Take out the fishing pole toy and let the cat do some captures to build confidence. If you do that close to the litterbox, the cat will transfer these feelings of confidence to the box.

And remember that litterbox problems might take a little bit of time to solve, especially if they've gone on for a while. Sometimes clients are sheepish about the fact that they didn't really mind that their cat went to the bathroom other places than the litterbox but then a new partner moved in or a child started complaining and demanding that the problem be fixed. If that's the case, it might take

more than a few days, but with patience you should still be able to succeed.

But when nothing else works, I tell clients about crate training. Borrow a big dog crate and put your cat in it with a litterbox, food and water. This compels the cat to use the litterbox in order to avoid sitting in his own pee. Whenever the cat uses the litter box, let him out for a few minutes as a reward. The time out of the crate should be tied to the reward for using the box. Increase the amount of time he's out of the crate with each use of the litterbox. As you do this, he'll get more comfortable with the idea of using it. This technique is more hardcore than I would like, but it's almost foolproof. And being a little bit hardcore is OK with me if it means a cat can avoid losing his home.

Midnight Sky

SAVING THE WORLD, ONE CAT AT A TIME

~*13*~

Scratch That

My cat is ruining the furniture and the carpets with scratching! How do I get her to stop?

This is another of the most common questions my clients ask me. "How do I keep my cat from scratching?"

The first thing I tell them is, you can't. Nor should you. Cats are meant to scratch. It is good for them and it serves an important purpose. In fact, it serves more than one important purpose. It sloughs off dead

Santana

By Rachel S. Geller, Ed.D.

Mia

cells from their claws, but it also carries a critical emotional component. When cats scratch, it releases their tension and anxiety. It makes them feel good. It also creates beneficial stretching for their back and neck muscles. For all of these reasons, we actually want cats to scratch. We just don't want them to scratch furniture or carpets.

My first question for clients who complain about scratching is whether they have a scratching post, and if so, what kind. Sometimes the choices that seem most obvious are not appropriate. One very popular choice is a scratching post covered with carpet. People choose these because they can pick out the particular scratching post that matches their color scheme.

But from a cat's point of view, a carpet on a scratching post is useless. It's not the ideal texture for them, and sometimes their claws get stuck in the loops. If this happens to your cat, you can be certain he will never use that scratching post again. A scratching post should be

SAVING THE WORLD, ONE CAT AT A TIME

covered with either sisal or rope. That's the best surface from which cats can get all the benefits of scratching with none of the risks.

And the next factor to consider is the height of the post. Often in clients' homes I see posts that are too short, like twelve to eighteen inches high. Your cat does not want to slouch or contort himself to scratch. To get the tension-releasing benefits of a good stretch, a cat needs to be able to reach up at least three feet on the scratching post.

Finally, the scratching post needs to be sturdy, with a wide solid base. If the scratching post feels wobbly or actually falls, your cat will not want to use it. But if you have the right scratching post – a proper surface, an appropriate height, a reliable base – your scratching problem will be solved.

Rosie

One other factor to consider is that some cats like to scratch horizontally rather than vertically. If your cat is a horizontal scratcher rather than a vertical one, look for a scratching pad – again, covered in rope or sisal and not carpet loops – instead of a post.

By Rachel S. Geller, Ed.D.

But of course, by the time my clients ask me for help with the scratching problem, the cat has generally already developed a habit of scratching furniture or carpets. So how do you get the cat to change an established behavior? Once you've set up your new scratching post or pad, play with your cat near it. You can lay the post on its side and run the fishing pole toy along the post. Eventually, in the course of play, the cat will sink her claws into the new pad or post and find it appealing. You could also try rubbing a little bit of catnip on the post.

Molly

Suppose you have a cat who scratches a couch or armchair. How do you change this behavior? It requires a two-pronged approach: make the couch or chair less appealing while introducing the post or scratching pad.

To make the furniture unappealing, think of these two adjectives: sticky and slick. Those are the two textures cats like least. Cover the furniture that the cat has been scratching with something like a carpet runner with the nubby side up – which will feel sticky – or put some kind

SAVING THE WORLD, ONE CAT AT A TIME

of plastic cover over the furniture – slick. Double-sided tape is a good deterrent also.

But don't only deter the cat from scratching the wrong thing: At the same time, redirect him to the right thing. Put your new scratching post or pad right next to where the cat was previously scratching. Picture your cat walking over to his favorite couch, finding it covered with slippery plastic, and then seeing the scratching post right next to it. He should quickly transfer his scratching tendencies from the unappealing object to the appealing one, as long as you present both at the same time.

Tuffy

By Rachel S. Geller, Ed.D.

~14~

Let's Take It Indoors

I've heard that cats are safer and healthier if kept indoors, but I know other people who say they can't imagine confining their cats in this way. What's the best choice on indoors versus outdoors?

Scarlet

I feel strongly that domesticated cats should be kept indoors. I understand feral cats in colonies are happier outdoors, but domesticated tame cats should be inside. They depend on people for food and shelter and care. They are not safe outside, where they face a far-reaching array of dangers:

SAVING THE WORLD, ONE CAT AT A TIME

Extreme cold. Coyotes. Cars. Diseases and parasites. Other cats, who are likely to be territorial.

Some people tell me that their cat scratches at the door and meows discontentedly if he is kept inside. I try to explain that this is not a sign the cat would be happier outside. Cats find it stressful to be outside, exposed to numerous hazards. But cats are very territorial. If they've spent some time outside, they become aware of other cats around. They want to monitor their territory and keep an eye on potential rivals who might be bigger, tougher and more dominant. That's a lot of work for them, and it doesn't make them happy. The comforts of indoor life make them happy. In fact, the life span of an indoor cat is sixteen to eighteen years; that's about twice as long as an outdoor cat.

What cats do like about the outdoors is all the stimuli. Cats are intelligent animals who like mental stimulation. So in

Nemo

order to keep your cat happy indoors, where he will be safer, you need to provide that. Engage your cat in playing

BY RACHEL S. GELLER, ED.D.

with an interactive toy like a fishing pole at least twice a day for at least fifteen minutes each time. And furnish solo toys for when you are not home, even something as simple as a tissue box with a ball inside.

Set up a window perch – which could be a window seat or a couch or bookshelf close to the window – so that your cat can see what's going on outside. Some cats like to watch TV. Of course, a second cat is another good source of stimulation. Provide enough ways for cats to stay active, stimulated and engaged, and they are not going to have the desire to go outside.

Sparkle

SAVING THE WORLD, ONE CAT AT A TIME

~15~

We Need to See Other People

How do I make my long-time cat comfortable with my new boyfriend?

Not all of the questions I get involve behavioral issues. Sometimes clients come to me because they are introducing a new person into their household – a

Taz

partner or spouse is moving in; a new roommate has been found – and they want to know how to make it work for both parties, feline and human alike.

83

By Rachel S. Geller, Ed.D.

The best way to bond with a cat is through the kind of interactive play therapy I've described earlier. When you interactively play and the cat is having fun and feeling great, all the positive associations are going to be associated with the person doing the play. So have the new person play with the cat.

Sparky and Roberta

But what if the cat is genuinely afraid of the new person? What if the cat runs away whenever that person walks into the room?

Have that new person find a spot where he can stand without the cat acting hostile to his presence, no matter how far away that is. The person should stay in that zone, ignoring the cat, acting indifferent, checking emails or reading or whatever. Then after a short time, he should walk away. Repeat that for several days, gradually adding more sessions and lengthening their duration. Eventually the cat will learn he is safe in the proximity of that person. Then the new person

SAVING THE WORLD, ONE CAT AT A TIME

can move a little bit closer and do the same thing. Every few days, move closer and closer. Then start playing with the fishing pole toy.

What a new person should not do when meeting a resistant cat is walk straight toward the cat. From a cat's perspective, this is predatory. Let the cat come to you, and when she does, don't make a big fuss. That would startle the cat and also send a signal that what she is doing is a big deal, and you don't want to reinforce that. Act nonchalant, so that the cat finds you nonthreatening.

When you bring someone new into the household, be sure your cat has plenty of safe spaces: perches, cat trees, maybe a cat tunnel. Let the cat go at his own pace in becoming acquainted with the new person. When the cat sees the new person as trustworthy, the relationship will progress at its own pace.

Abagail

85

BY RACHEL S. GELLER, ED.D.

~16~

It's All in the Training

Can any of this advice really change the way my cat behaves?

Selma

One of the greatest myths about cats is that they have independent natures. I disagree with that descriptor. Cats are independent hunters, as opposed to dogs which hunt in packs, but they are not independent in the emotional sense. They want attention and love from the people around them.

SAVING THE WORLD, ONE CAT AT A TIME

Cat owners say to me all the time, "My cat is like a dog." They mean that their cat meets them at the door, follows them around the house, and wants to sit

Princess

on their lap. The stereotype of cats as solitary loners is so pervasive that everyone whose cat is not like this thinks their cat is unique. But the fact is that cats love proximity and attention. For this reason, it's only natural that they greet their owners at the door, follow us around the house, sit on a computer or newspaper while we are working or reading. They depend on us for food and shelter, but also for comfort, affection and mental stimulation.

Another misconception is the idea that you cannot train a cat. In reality, you can train cats the same way you train dogs: with a clicker or with food. Many cats are quite motivated by edible treats. Like with a dog, you can get your cat to do very specific actions like sit down or shake paws. More importantly, you can train your cats to do useful things like enter their carriers before a trip out of the house or go to their cat beds when you want to go to sleep.

BY RACHEL S. GELLER, ED.D.

For example, if you want to train your cat to go into the carrier, the best way is for a treat in the carrier to serve as a cue. But first, leave the carrier in the middle of the room, line it with favorite blankets, and open the door. Make it cozy and appealing for the cat. Put treats inside the carrier for your cat to discover once he does go in.

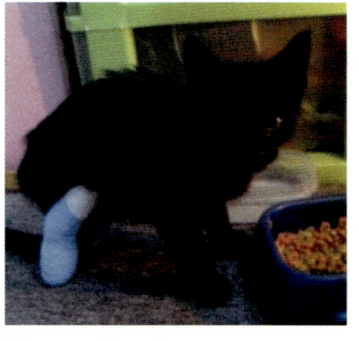

Marcus Maurice

Then when your cat enters the carrier by choice, close the carrier door for five minutes. Let the cat see that there's no harm in it. Do this for several days in a row. Eventually when the cat sees the carrier with the door open, he will know there's probably a snack awaiting him inside, and nothing to be feared by venturing in.

One thing many of my clients want to train their cat not to do is jump up onto the kitchen counter. I tell them to start by figuring out what about the counter appeals to the cat. Is there food on the counter? Does he feel safer off the floor, perhaps away from another cat? Is there a stimulating view he likes?

Each of these incentives can be counteracted. If it's because of food, then try not to keep food on the counter. If

SAVING THE WORLD, ONE CAT AT A TIME

you think another pet might be intimidating your cat, be sure your pets have vertical cat trees or other perches with which to establish their own territory and someplace to which they can escape. And try to put cat trees or perches near a window, so that cats can take an interest in what's going on outside.

The other piece of the countertop puzzle is giving your cats a disincentive to jumping up onto the counter. Once you've removed any incentives to be there or redirected the cat's interest elsewhere, try putting a temporary surface on your counter that the cat will find unappealing. As with my instructions about how to prevent cats from scratching carpets or furniture, think slick or sticky as the two surfaces cats will avoid. You might try covering the counter with a carpet runner turned to expose

the nubby side, or with some shiny slippery contact paper. And again, remember that if your cat is to learn not to jump on the counter, he'll need

Spirit

By Rachel S. Geller, Ed.D.

an appealing alternative, like a perch or cat tree near a window.

Some cat owners use squirt bottles to train cats out of undesirable behaviors, but I don't advocate that. Your cat will associate you with something unpleasant and will become afraid of you, which isn't a good goal. You'll have a wet cat who will try to circumvent you and who will fear you, without any positive motivation to change his behavior. Moreover, he might just save the bad behaviors such as scratching or jumping onto the counters for when you're not home, which hasn't solved the problem.

Milliesweet

SAVING THE WORLD, ONE CAT AT A TIME

~17~

Calling In Sick

You've talked about a lot of behavioral issues, but what if the problem is medical? How will I know if something is really wrong?

As with many animals, feeling physically unwell gives cats an unwelcome sense of vulnerability. Therefore, even with their trusted owners, they will try to hide the fact that they are sick.

Triton

So as a cat owner, you need to be vigilant about physical symptoms. You know what your cat looks like and

acts like when healthy: he eats, drinks, plays, grooms, uses the litterbox. Changes in any of these behaviors are cause for concern.

Be aware of changes in your cat's personality as well. If she is usually playful but becomes lethargic; if she is typically gregarious but seems to be hiding from you or withdrawing from you; if she is sleeping more than usual; even persistent meowing are all reasons to consider the possibility of illness.

Of course, physical symptoms of illness, such as nose or eye discharge, sneezing, or coughing are sometimes the easiest clues to spot. No matter what, if you are concerned, make an appointment to see your vet. Cats should also have regular check-ups at least once a year, and more as they get older, after the age of nine years old or so.

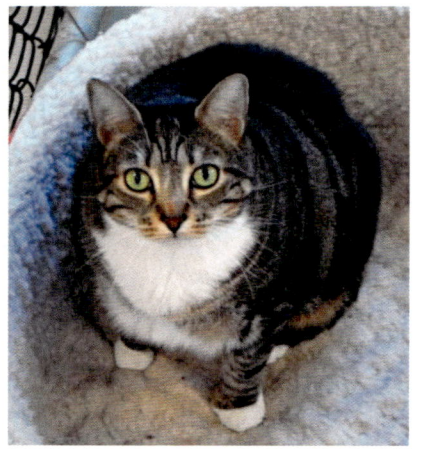

Tyson

SAVING THE WORLD, ONE CAT AT A TIME

~*18*~

The Hard Work of Saying Goodbye

Recently I underwent certification to become a Pet Chaplain with the Association for Veterinary Pastoral Education. After devoting so much of my time to animal welfare, this seemed like the next logical step to me. Cats

Minnie

simply have much shorter lifespans than humans, so inevitably, I've seen many of my human clients lose their pets, and of course I've lost many pets myself.

Moreover, many of the clients I work with have elderly cats, because problems – particularly litterbox problems, but also issues around introducing new cats into

93

By Rachel S. Geller, Ed.D.

the household – often correlate to having an older pet. So a large number of the cats I work with are about eight or older.

Adding chaplaincy to my skill set meant that I could not only help people with their cats' behavior but also help them to cope with the sorrows of losing a pet. It was another tool for my toolkit. One of my first discoveries as I underwent chaplaincy training was that when someone needs counseling after losing a pet, often what they most need to do is talk about their pet. My role is to sit by their side and take the journey with them, not have a two-way

Bebe

dialogue in which I sympathize by telling them about my own experiences with losing pets. My focus as a chaplain needs to be completely on the person I am helping.

When I work with a bereaved person, I ask that person to tell me a favorite story about the cat. As we talk, I can see how comforting it is for the owner to remember those solid bonds and review the experiences they had with their cat. So my first piece of advice for someone coping

SAVING THE WORLD, ONE CAT AT A TIME

with the loss of a pet is to either tell or write down all your favorite memories of your cat: funny habits the cat had, things you liked to do together, times that your cat made you laugh.

One grieving client told me that her recently deceased cat was like a little brother to her. I asked her to explain why that was. She described how he'd

Jack

follow her around the house, and when she did yoga he'd roll onto his back as if he was imitating her. As she told me the stories, I saw her beginning to smile, taking comfort from these happy memories.

I also encourage people to create a memorial or shrine to their cat. Sometimes this takes the form of framed photos of the cat; other times it's a collection of the cat's favorite toys or even the cat's bed. All of this is helpful in that it forges a continuing bond between the person and their pet.

Sometimes what people most need from me is not any one approach – stories, shrines – but just tacit permission to grieve their pet as they would a person. As I

BY RACHEL S. GELLER, ED.D.

think I've made clear, I've always been someone who saw the cats in the household as equally important and valued as the people, and most of my clients feel the same way, but their own family members or friends, even close friends, might not. So sometimes all they need is for me to make them feel comfortable grieving their pet in whatever way they need to do. Maybe that even means holding a memorial service of some kind. If that kind of ritual can bring them comfort, I absolutely encourage it.

Tuffy

For myself, I like to keep tangible reminders of each cat in the form of ashes displayed in marble urns. One of the perks of being a rabbi's daughter is that in the past I've had contacts at some funeral homes, where I've purchased beautiful marble urns. As I've lost cats over the years, I've had each one cremated and put the ashes in an urn; then I engrave the urn with the cat's name and some special words that remind me of the cat. Usually that's a phrase that I often said when I spoke to the cat. For example, Tuffy's urn says "Such a good boy," which is

how I always described him. Muffin's urn says "Cutest cat in the whole world." I've also done plantings in honor of my cats, to create a living memorial for them at my home: a birch tree for Minnie and a rose garden to honor Rosie.

The other thing I've done for my cats is created legacies in their honor. Tuffy had cardiomyopathy, so when he passed away, I established the Tuffy Fund at a particular shelter so that it would have resources to take in cats with chronic illnesses. When Minnie

Minnie and Rosie

passed away, I established a fund at The Cat Connection to help build a new cat shelter in her honor, appropriately named the Minnie Fund. My husband and I also made a donation to Angell Memorial Hospital and had a tree of life leaf created there in honor of Muffin, Tuffy, Minnie and Rosie.

Most recently, my chaplaincy work led me to a woman whose dog had recently passed away after a very

BY RACHEL S. GELLER, ED.D.

long life – the dog lived well into the high teens, which particularly for a small dog is unusual. The woman is single and lives by herself; her dog was her primary companion.

Sochi

She and I had several hourlong sessions and covered a lot of ground. Much of our conversation centered around her overwhelming sense of loss in general, but also more specifically the sense that many of her friends didn't understand how she could be experiencing so much grief over someone who was, in their words, "just a dog." She admitted she even misses visits to the vet and all the other relationships she had developed in relation to her dog's life. There were so many layers to her loss.

During one session, when my client was immersed in thoughts of how sad and lonely she felt without her dog, she told me that she still had the dog's beds around her house. Friends who visited kept urging her to dispose of them. They said it was unhealthy or otherwise inappropriate to keep the beds of a deceased dog around her home. But I assured her that it was fine for her to hold on to the beds for as long as she wanted to do so.

SAVING THE WORLD, ONE CAT AT A TIME

Then the conversation turned to other topics. But the next day, the client emailed me to say that she took particular comfort in my remark that she should feel she had permission to keep the dog beds. To me, it was such a simple issue and so easily

Boo Boo

resolved – of course she should keep the dog beds if she wanted to – but to her it was extremely validating and important. Her friends did not understand the sentimental value that these objects held for her, but I did. After all, when a person dies, it's not considered unusual or strange to hold on to something of theirs, clothing or jewelry or a book or a photo. I still have shirts that belonged to my father. And yet people didn't seem to think it was reasonable in the case of a dog.

But just my granting her reassurance that there was therapeutic value in holding on to these objects that she associated with her beloved dog helped her to feel better. And it made me feel grateful that she chose me to go through this journey with her and I was able to provide her with that comfort.

BY RACHEL S. GELLER, ED.D.

~19~

A Particularly Meaningful Success Story

Yodi

One client came to me from the Cat Connection, one of the shelters where I provide counseling services. She called the shelter and said she wanted to surrender her cat because at the age of seventeen, the cat didn't seem happy anymore. She said that the cat had recently started peeing outside of her litterbox and the woman felt

SAVING THE WORLD, ONE CAT AT A TIME

that the household had become too lively for the aging cat, so she felt the best thing to do would be to give her cat up.

I convinced her that the cat would surely be happier in a familiar household, no matter how many children were running around making noise, than in a strange shelter. I said the cat would rather have a little less attention than may be optimally desirable than moved to a strange place after seventeen years in the same house. I explained that cats are very perceptive, and that the cat could understand that the family needed to go about its regular activities, but that the cat is part of the family and families should stick together.

Timmy

I talked to her about how the kids could maybe approach the cat a little bit more calmly, without a lot of yelling and chasing, and that would make everyone feel better also. Addressing the litterbox problem, I told her that

101

BY RACHEL S. GELLER, ED.D.

older cats sometimes have trouble with the high sides of their litterboxes and maybe she just needed one with lower sides, or maybe there needed to be more litterboxes in the house because an older cat needs to pee more frequently and not travel so far to get to a litterbox.

She took my advice, changing the litterbox configuration and accepting my reassurance that the cat could cope with a little household chaos, and kept the cat. Three years later I received an email thanking me profusely. She said that the cat had lived to be twenty years old, and that the past three years had been happy and

Cody

meaningful for the pet and the family. She said she knew in her heart that she had done the right thing by listening to me, and she knew the cat's life had been better for it. It took her three years to tell me this, but I was still so gratified to know that I had saved the cat from what would have been a very unhappy fate.

SAVING THE WORLD, ONE CAT AT A TIME

~20~

I'm Here for You

A woman contacted me for advice on adopting a stray cat into her house. I encouraged her to trap the cat and bring it in. The cat was tremendously anxious and mistrustful. I worked with the client for six months or more just trying to acclimate the cat to the woman's presence. It was baby steps all the way. Progress after several months meant the cat sitting ten feet away from her.

Finally, she emailed me to say that she

Smokey

felt generally comfortable with how things were going. The cat wasn't affectionate, but he seemed at least comfortable

By Rachel S. Geller, Ed.D.

living with her. A couple of weeks later she emailed me again with startling news. Though she hadn't mentioned it earlier, during the time she'd been trying to acclimate the cat, a second stray cat had started showing up at her doorstep. She definitely didn't want to bring in a second cat while she still had such a long way to go with the first, but she was starting to feel like maybe it was time to allow the second cat in, because he seemed friendly and because cold weather was approaching.

So she let the cat in but carefully kept the two cats separated. Then one day one of them escaped his barrier. He walked over to the other cat and they stared at each other, then meowed and chirped as if starting a

Tiger

conversation. It truly seemed as if they recognized each other, she said. The two cats trotted off into another room and lay down together.

And after that, the first cat started behaving much more gregariously toward her, no longer shy and withdrawn. So now the woman had a household with two friendly cats – all because she'd taken a chance on

SAVING THE WORLD, ONE CAT AT A TIME

acclimating one stray into her house, with my guidance. It made both of us feel great that we'd saved two cats together.

As a cat behavior therapist and a cat shelter supporter, my primary goal is always to help people work through problems with their cats such that cats can stay in the homes to which they've been adopted rather than returning to a shelter.

Sometimes I feel like a psychotherapist or a pediatrician, though, when it comes to the urgency of the calls I occasionally receive. Unfortunately, I do not always possess the same skills of objectivity and dissociation that therapists and physicians develop over years of training. In other words, I tend to take my work personally. I want cats to be safe and loved; I want cat owners to be happy with their pets.

Flower

By Rachel S. Geller, Ed.D.

Minnie

And so I go the extra mile for my clients, because I'm so emotionally invested in my work. Sometimes my efforts pay off. I have hundreds of emails, phone messages and photos from past clients thanking me for the help I provided to them in integrating their cats into their lives.

But I'm no different from any other professional in that I can't be successful one hundred percent of the time. One Sunday evening I was at home in my pajamas at around nine o'clock when my phone rang. The caller, who had gotten my number from a shelter, was in a panic. He had just adopted a cat and the cat was refusing to use the litterbox. The man's wife had said if the cat didn't start using the litterbox, she was going to move out. He was crying as he told me this, pleading for help, saying he didn't want to give up either the cat or his wife.

He lived a half-hour from me, but I was so distressed by his story that I got dressed and prepared to

SAVING THE WORLD, ONE CAT AT A TIME

drive to his house. Before I did, though, I said to him, "Would your wife be willing to work with a cat behaviorist if I assure her I can fix this problem as long as you give me a little time?" I wanted at least his verbal assurance that this effort would be worth my while. He promised me that his wife would be open to my advice.

At 10 p.m. I arrived at their home. Although it was a large house, I discovered that the litterbox had been placed on the third floor that was little more than an attic annex, a dark, damp, unpleasant place.

Baby

The cat had to take a hike just to find the litterbox, and this was a brand new cat who probably wasn't even feeling brave enough to explore the house yet. It was an easy problem to identify.

I talked to the couple and looked around the house with them; together we identified several better locations for the litterbox. I told them I was one hundred percent confident that if they moved the litterbox to a convenient, accessible spot, the problem would be solved in no more

By Rachel S. Geller, Ed.D.

than a couple of days, as soon as the cat became familiar with the litterbox's new location.

The husband was happy and the wife was agreeable. I told them they were welcome to email me any time, but I honestly didn't think they'd need to. It was such an easy fix.

It was midnight when I arrived home, but I felt great. I fell asleep believing I'd just saved both a cat and a marriage.

When I awoke the next morning, I found a voicemail on my cellphone sent three hours earlier, around dawn. The man said that as soon as I left, his wife had a change of heart and started packing her suitcase, saying that

Blanche

she couldn't stay another moment with the cat. Of course the man capitulated – though I'm not sure I would have if I were him! – and told his wife to stay; the cat would go. And he brought the cat back to the shelter.

I felt so dejected. Returning to the shelter is so traumatizing for a cat. They

don't like change anyway; and to be taken from a shelter to a home and back to the shelter must have been tremendously stressful. I cried at how this situation had turned out.

The point of this story is that I can help anyone with a cat problem as long as they are willing to give me a chance. I can't

Sophie and Phoebus

solve the problem with a wave of a magic wand, but it's quite likely I can fix it with some time and with clients who are willing to work with me and follow my recommendations. Some problems need more time than others to solve. We can take small steps along the way. I can help make the relationship between you and your cat succeed if you just give me the chance, which this couple had not done.

I was heartbroken, but the story had a happy ending for the cat. She was adopted a week later into a different household. Her new owner still sends me pictures of this cat, who went through far too many changes in far too little time but now has a happy life.

By Rachel S. Geller, Ed.D.

Please be patient with your cat. Almost all cat problems have solutions. They may just take time and effort and patience to solve. But once you solve them, you will be rewarded with one of the most wonderful relationships you have ever known.

What's your cat story? Did you solve a problem on your own? Did you use one of the solutions I've described in this book to improve your life with your cat? Have you figured out an approach that I haven't discussed? I'm always interested in learning more about cats and their owners. Please contact me at www.DrRachelCatBehavior.com. I wish you and all of your pets the very best!

SAVING THE WORLD, ONE CAT AT A TIME

ABOUT THE AUTHORS

RACHEL S. GELLER, ED.D., spent over 20 years as a special education teacher in the Waltham public schools. After retiring from a career in education, she became a Certified Humane Education Specialist and a Cat Behavior and Retention Specialist through the Humane Society of the United States as well as a Certified Pet Chaplain through the Association for Veterinary Pastoral Education. She serves as a cat behavior specialist at several Boston-area cat shelters including the Cat Connection in Waltham, where she is on the Board of Directors; the Baypath Humane Society in Hopkinton; and the Here Today Adopted Tomorrow Animal Sanctuary in Brimfield. To learn more, go to www.DrRachelCatBehavior.com.

NANCY SHOHET WEST is a Boston-area journalist who helps individuals, multi-generational families, communities, and special interest groups to write and self-publish their memoirs. For more information, go to www.NancyShohetWest.com.

Made in the USA
Las Vegas, NV
02 September 2021

29463396R00071

About the Author

Courtesy Joan Lipkin.

Ann Lemons Pollack has been writing about food a good while, but not so long that she remembers all the restaurants in this book. A picky eater as a child growing up in Desloge, Missouri, she came out of her shell with a vengeance.

She's reviewed restaurants, written cooking columns, traveled for food and was daring enough to cook for and then marry the restaurant critic of the *St. Louis Post-Dispatch*, Joe Pollack. Together, they wrote three guidebooks to St. Louis food and many food and travel stories. Ann carries on the tradition and is currently found monthly in and online at *St. Louis Magazine* and on her blog, stlouiseats.typepad.com, where she also writes about theater.

Index

Rinaldi, Jack 29
Robyn, Charles 26
Rogers, Will 17, 27
Rorer, Sarah Tyson 17, 19
Rossino's 82
Ross, Steve 31
Roth, William 53
Rovak, Abe 69
Rozelle, Pete 111
Ruggeri, Antonio 85
Ruggeri, Henry (Henrico) 85
Ruggeri, Minnie (Ermina) 85
Ruggeri's Restaurant 85
Russo Del Pietro, Mary Rose 83
Russo, Roy and Nina 83
Russo Zimmerman, Nancy and Tom Zimmerman 83

S

Saigh, Bill and Christine 57
Savan, Glenn 34
Schnaider, Joseph 87
Schnaider's Beer Garden 87
Schneithorst, Arthur and Bertha 106
Schuchard, Pat and Carol 108
Shu Feng 48
Sinatra, Frank 102
Speropoulos, Jimmy 62
Springsteen, Bruce 28
Stan Musial and Biggie's Steak House 90
Stern, Isaac 28
Sting (Gordon Sumner) 85
Stockton, J. Roy 66
Storck, Shelby 37
Sunshine Inn, The 92, 119
Sweeney, Ray 29

T

Three Fountains, The 93
Timney, David 29
Tony Faust's Oyster House & Restauant 95
Toothman, Ben and Elmer 45
Toothman, James and Mary 44
Tucci, Kim 85
Two Cents Plain 51
Tyrolean Alps Restauant 15

V

Vacho, Pierre 37
Vonk, Hans 55
Voss, Jimmy 34

W

Warner, Kirk 55, 116
White, Andy 29
Wilcox, Agnes 25
Wild, Art 97
Wild's Palace of Poison 97
Wolf, Don 49

Y

Young, Bryan 29

Z

Zinnia 98

INDEX

McCormack, John 17
McDowell, Cary 56
McGinley, Lou Ellen 76
McGinley, William L. 73
McGuire, John 56
McGuire, Matt 55
McIntyre, Steve 28
Medart, Bill 64
Medart's 64
Mertikas, Jim 42
Miller, Lester 27
Miller, Mitch 28
Miss Hulling's 65
Mormino, Frank 37
Mosberger, Greg 54
Mostel, Zero 28
Murray, Bill 111
Musial, Stan 25, 27, 90
Mutrux, George 95
Mutrux, Michelle 95
Mutrux, Paul 94
Mutrux, Richard 94

N

Nantucket Cove 68, 117
Naugle, Dick 71
Naugles Tacos and Burgers 71
Neal, Gary 103
Newman, Paul 28
Nickens, Rudy 93
Noah's Ark 72

P

Palace of Poison 97
Papadimos, Aris 43
Parkmoor 73, 118
Pelican, Demetrios James and
    Katharine 77
Pelican's Cafe 77
Perlman, Itzhak 56
Perry, Richard 53
Politis, Lou and Bill 62
Politis, Pete and Alex 62
Ponticello, Angelo and Rose 79
Ponticello, Frank 80
Ponticello Reiss, Vicki and Ludwig
    Reiss 80
Ponticello's Restaurant 79
Ponticello, Vito and Rose 79
Potts, Frank and Charlie 70
Powers, Ron 78
Profeta, Gabriella 40
Profeta, Peppe 40
Profeta, Salvatore 40

R

recipes
    Elsah Landing Pumpkin Praline
        Pie 113
    Fio's La Fourchette 115
    Green Parrot Inn Fried Chicken
        116
    King Louie's Chilled Spiced
        Tomato-Pepper Soup 116
    Nantucket Cove Mayfair Dressing
        117
    Parkmoor's Chickburger 118
    Sunshine Inn Cheesy Italian
        Dressing 119
Redel, Lee 29
Rhomberg, Greg R. 79
Riddle's Penultimate 80

Index

Gian-Peppe's 40
Gibson, Bob 25
Gitto, Charlie 83
Goldman, Emma 96
Gontram, Bob 46
Gontram, Steve 46
Grecian Gardens 41, 64
Green Parrot Inn, The 44, 116
Griesedieck, Anton 77
Guempel, David 29, 98

H

Hanna, Saleem 79
Harvest 45
Heiss, Gordon 69
Hirt, Al 91
Holloran, Patrick 55
House of Maret, The 47
Hulling Apted, Florence 65

I

In Soo 48
Irv's Good Food 49

J

Jada (Jada Conforto) 52
Jefferson Avenue Boarding House 53
Jefferson, Joseph 96
Joyce, Dan 29
Jugaloff, Pete 109
Jung, In Soo 48

K

Kann, Stan 87, 90
Karandzieff, Andy 110
Karandzieff, Bessie De Polito 110
Karandzieff, George 109
Karandzieff, Harry 109
Karandzieff, Mike 110
Karandzieff, Tina (Athena) 109
Karandzieff, Tommy 110
Kelly, Edward 42
Kimmel, Jimmy 111
King Louie's 55, 117
Kirby, Tim 34

L

Lady Charles (Charles Perrine) 29, 38
LaRussa, Tony 55
Laskaris, Chris 77
Lettuce Leaf 57
Lindbergh, Charles 27
Lindgren, Dorothy 35
Little Italy 58
Louisiana Purchase Exposition 13
Lt. Robert E. Lee 59
Luchow, August 15

M

Mahe, George 46
Majestic Restaurant 62
Maret, Robert 47
Maret, Wilhelm and Barbara 47
McBroom, Martha 93
McCarthy, Jake 21

INDEX

Brynner, Yul 40
Buck, Jack 25, 108
Buente, George 26
Burroughs, William S. 32, 34
Busch, Adolphus 96
Busch, August A. 15, 106
Busch, August IV 56
Busch, John 26

C

Candicci, Bob 85
Caray, Harry 27
Carl, Jack 51
Channing, Carol 111
Chez Leon 30
Cisco's 33
Claiborne, Craig 95
Conway, Robert 79
Crafton, Helen 35
Crown Candy Kitchen 109
Curtis, Tony 111

D

Dailey, Adalaide 28
Del Pietro Doherty, Lea 83
Del Pietro, Marc 83
Del Pietro, Michael, Jr. 83
Del Pietro, Mike, Sr. 83
Devine, Karen 99
Dohack family 32
Dohack's Restaurant 32
Dolan, Cardinal Timothy 25
Dowd, Tena May 44
Downs, Carolyn 47
Downs, Charlie 46

Duff's 33
Duffy, Karen 34

E

Eagleton, Thomas 25, 49
Elsah Landing 35
Ettlinger, Nate 103
Europa 390 37

F

Faille, Mike 83
Faust, Anthony R. 15, 95
Faust, Anthony (son of Anthony R.) 77, 97
Faust, Edward 96
Ferrara, John 85
Fiore, Amadeo 83
Fio's La Fourchette 38
Flavan, David and John 72
Flynn, Tom 30
Fonda, Henry 102
Ford, Selena 29
Forgione, Larry 23
Fresta, Joe 85
Fung, Steve 48

G

Gallagher, Sean 29
Garagiola, Joe 86, 90
Garagiola, Mickey 86, 90
Garagnani, Julius 90
Georges, Pete, John and George 42
Gianino, Frank 83

Index

A

Adams, Larry 98
Adams, Maude 96
Al's Restaurant 101
Anscheutz, Carl 77
Antognini, Fio 38, 115
Antognini, Lisa 38
Apted, Stephen J. 65, 66
Apted, Stephen R. 66
Ayers, Andy 81
Ayers, K.T. (Katherine) 82
Ayers, Paula 81

B

Baker, Al 21, 49
Baker, Mary 21
Balaban, Herb 28
Balaban's 28
Balsano, Dick 91
Bardolinos 85

Baroni, Al, Jr. 102
Baroni, Al, Sr. 101
Baroni, Louise 101
Baroni Neal, Pam 103
Barrymore famiy 96
Beffa's 24
Belshaw, Jim 54
Bennett, Tony 28
Berra, John 86
Berra, Yogi (Lawrence P.) 85, 86
Bevo, Das 108
Bevo Mill 77, 104
Bidwill, Billy 111
Bierbaum, Leon 30
Boettigheimer McDowell, Holly 56
Bommarito, Vince 25
Bourdain, Anthony 34
Bousquet, Matthew 46
Breneman Medart, Blossom 64
Brock, Lou 25
Bruno, Giovanna 58
Bruno, Mario 58
Bruno's Little Italy 59

Suggested Reading

It will be obvious in reading this book that I made considerable use of newspaper archives. Newspapers are invaluable for this sort of thing: accounts that aren't viewed through the mists of time, but written fresh. Even advertisements contribute something.

Here are some other things to read if you're interested.

Crone, Thomas. *Gaslight Square: "An Oral History."* St. Louis, MO: The William and Joseph Press, 2004.

Oldani, John L., PhD. *Sweetness Preserved: The Story of the Crown Candy Kitchen.* St. Louis, MO: Virginia Press, 2005.

Terry, Elizabeth. *Oysters to Angus: Three Generations of the St. Louis Faust Family.* St. Louis, MO: Bluebird Publishing, 2014.

Vaccaro, Pamela J. *Beyond the Ice Cream Cone: The Whole Scoop on Food at the 1904 World's Fair.* St. Louis, MO: Enid Press, 2004.